Have a Love Affair with the USA

"*Have a Love Affair with the USA* is a beautiful reminder that America's greatest strength lives in its people: their stories, struggles, and shared hopes. As Evelyn and Natalie Kelly travel across all 50 states, they reveal a nation rich in history, resilience, and heart. Their travel tips, which you won't find on any search engine, reflect something I deeply believe: when we travel with curiosity, respect, and an open mind, we don't just see new places, we come to better understand one another. This book invites readers to rediscover America and to reconnect with the values that bind us together."

–**Senator Darryl Rouson- Florida State Senate, Attorney, Author**

"For decades, I've enjoyed reading travel books. This is the first one I've ever read that passionately describes America. Now, I'll return to places already visited with refreshed insight and plan new trips to come. Along with my copy, I'll buy one for each of my kids. I bet it will guide their family travel for years to come. Bravo, Evelyn and Natalie, for sharing your love affair with travel for all of us to enjoy!"

–**Dr. Kevin Singer. PhD, former school administrator and world traveler**

"This book is a fun and most informative read. The mother and daughter authors play off each other and deliver a reading that conjures images across our wonderful country, engaging, insightful, and crisp... they make you want to go there and check it out for yourself."

–**Dr. Casius Pealer II, PhD. Emeritus college administrator, Central Florida College**

"I've been traveling across the U.S. since I was two years old—and yet, page after page, this book introduced me to places and stories I'd never seen. It's as if someone opened a hidden map of America and said, 'Come look behind the curtain.'

As a lifelong teacher, author, and intuitive, I trust the power of a feeling—and my intuition says this is a keeper. The kind of book that makes you dream, plan, and pack. This isn't just a travel book. It's a beautifully curated call to adventure.

"If you love America, if you long to explore it more deeply—or if you're simply ready for new inspiration—this book is a treasure. One I'll be gifting often." Written by explorers who've seen 89 countries, their lens on America is both grounded and full of wonder. They're pointing us in the right direction—and what a direction it is."

–Rev. Nancy Orlen Weber, R.N. Author, podcaster, psychic detective

"The Kellys—Evelyn and Natalie—do it again! In *Have A Love Affair with the USA*, the dynamic writing duo offers readers and all travel enthusiasts a comprehensive yet light-hearted reminder of why America is the greatest country in the world. *Have A Love Affair with the USA* is a delightful read to be enjoyed by all."

–Dr. John Smith, PhD- University administrator and professor, author, speaker

"As someone who loved their first book, I couldn't wait to dive into *Have a Love Affair with the USA* and they've done it again with another gem! This isn't just a travel book; it's a heartfelt journey through the landscapes, history, culture, and quirks that make America so extraordinary. I especially appreciate how the authors weave together captivating stories, little-known historical facts, smart travel tips, and all while spotlighting hidden treasures only locals know about. Whether you're a seasoned traveler, an armchair explorer, or someone planning your first adventure across the U.S., this book is for you. It's a celebration of the human spirit and the beauty of our nation. Perfect for families, road trippers, history buffs, and anyone curious about what makes America special. With every page, you're reminded that adventure, inspiration, and connection are often just around the corner. Highly recommend!"

–Malia Rogers, Founder of MediGap Pros LLC & #1 Amazon Best Selling Author of *Magnetic Allure*, world-class speaker.

Have a Love Affair with the USA

Have a Love Affair with the USA

Discover USA's Beauty, Humor, and Hidden Gems

Evelyn Kelly Ph.D. and
Natalie Kelly M.S.

Published by Travelersatheart.com

ISBN (paperback): 979-8-9917211-2-7
ISBN (ebook): 979-8-9917211-3-4

Book design and production by www.AuthorSuccess.com
Front cover by www.adobestock.com

Printed in the United States of America

To Charles L. Kelly (1929-2020)
and all the Kelly family, children, grandchildren,
great-grandchildren

"Let the good times roll."

Contents

Introduction

Have a Love Affair with the USA: Discover USA's Beauty, Humor, & Hidden Gems

When people learn that we've traveled to 89 countries and 50 states, they often ask, "What's your favorite country?" Without hesitation, we answer: The United States of America. In fact, having explored the world makes us say it louder and with greater conviction. This book is about the United States of America and falling in love with its natural wonders, layers of history, and the resilience and creativity of its people.

The USA isn't just a country on the map; it's a living story. It offers a tremendous variety of landscapes, communities, and experiences. Every state has its own personality, shaped by geography, culture, and innovation. Together, our 50 states form a patchwork quilt that is unique yet united: the United States of America.

While popular theme parks are fun, they don't have to be the only stops for a family vacation. And while Europe has its treasures, we don't always need a passport or a long flight to find adventure. Some of the most unforgettable experiences are right here in our own backyard, across this remarkable nation.

In *Have a Love Affair with the USA*, we invite you to travel with us from sea to shining sea. Like our earlier book, *Have a Love Affair with Travel*, this isn't a traditional guidebook. Instead, it's a celebration of the human spirit told through stories that inspire, surprise, and remind us how extraordinary America, and life itself, can be.

Why Travel the USA?

We travel to the USA because every trip reveals something new. Mountains remind us of strength. Rivers show us change and flow. Small towns capture the heart of the community. Big cities hum with energy. Our nation's stories, some triumphant and some painful, reveal who we are and what we strive to become. Whether you're a seasoned road-tripper, an armchair traveler, or someone dreaming of your next escape, this book can spark your own love affair with the USA. Adventure, beauty, and wonder are closer than you think.

How This Book Is Organized

This book shares seventy-nine stories across six themed parts. At the end of each story, we include a SMART TIP, a practical piece of advice. But the book is more than a collection of adventures. It offers tips for smarter and stress-free trips, based on our personal experiences and insights from fellow travelers.

What This Book Will Do for You:

- Find hidden gems and iconic landmarks. From quirky small towns with unforgettable names to world-famous wonders, discover stories that bring places to life.
- Explore history you can touch. Walk alongside pioneers, immigrants, and visionaries who shaped our nation.
- Flavor culture and food adventures. Taste the USA through regional specialties, food traditions, and the surprising history behind the dishes we love.
- Inspire you to travel. Whether planning a cross-country road trip or exploring from your favorite chair, you'll gather ideas, tips, and sparks of curiosity.
- Celebrate the American spirit. Meet everyday people whose resilience, creativity, and humor embody the heart and promise of the United States.

Evelyn and Natalie Kelly

PART 1

America the Beautiful

The USA is home to breathtaking destinations that rival any place on earth. This chapter explores several icons and then celebrates the National Parks, the most fantastic idea America has ever had.

Leaf Peeping:
A Colorful Obsession

Going to See the Leaves

Living in Central **Florida**, we feel the heat lingering well into October. A group packs their bags and begins an extraordinary, soul-stirring journey to East **Tennessee**.

It always struck us as funny that people travel miles to look at leaves. Surely, there's more to it than that. But they return energized, inspired, and claiming something near a spiritual experience.

And Now for the Shock: Leaf Peeping

We first encountered this curious term in 2024, while on a tour of six New England states. The timing was perfect for us to catch the foliage at peak color. We *didn't* expect to be told we'd be "leaf peeping."

We may have misunderstood, so we asked the guide to repeat it twice. *LEAF PEEPING?* Perhaps it was the New England accent that threw us off. We knew what a leaf was, of course, but "peep"? That word had strange associations. We thought of "Peeping Toms," those sneaky characters lurking outside windows, or "peep show," which was not about trees.

Made in the USA

Somewhere in all this color, the term *leaf peeping* was born.

In 1966, Vermont's *Bennington Banner* popularized the phrase. Some say locals coined the term to describe the tourists who flood their towns every fall. Either way, the name stuck. And so, we found ourselves saying it too, *leaf peeping, and laughing all the way.*

Leaf tourism contributes over $20 billion to local economies across 24 eastern states. In fact, expect crowds and hope your guide knows how to avoid them. Our friends, the Pealers, recalled a bus trip where towns were so jammed that buses stretched in long lines just to get through. Even meals were served in 45-minute shifts, but the scenery of the six New England states is worth the wait.

Western Massachusetts

We loved Boston, but nothing prepared us for the beauty of the Berkshires. Drenched in autumn hues, the mountains looked like someone had thrown a patchwork quilt over the landscape. After visiting the Norman Rockwell Museum in Stockbridge, we rode on winding country roads, marveling at maples ablaze in crimson.

New England fall at its best: leaf peeping on Norman Rockwell's Stockbridge street, made even better by an 800-pound pumpkin stealing the show.

Connecticut

Connecticut in the fall is an artist's dream: a kaleidoscope of crimson, amber, gold, and russet. The hardwoods, rolling hills, and colonial charm make it one of New England's best leaf-peeping destinations.

Vermont

The hills of **Vermont** are alive with the Sound of Music. Tucked into the rolling hills of **Vermont** stands one of America's most unexpected cultural treasures, the Trapp Family Lodge, home of the real-life von Trapps whose story inspired *The Sound of Music.* Long before the sweeping Alps and soaring melodies became Hollywood legend, the family quietly built a new chapter of their lives here in New England.

After fleeing Austria during World War II, the von Trapps settled in **Vermont** in the 1940s, drawn to the familiar mountain landscape that reminded them of their beloved homeland. On a modest farm, they opened a small 27-room guesthouse—a humble beginning that, over generations, blossomed into a 2,600-acre alpine-style resort still welcoming travelers from around the world.

We were especially pleased to feel the pull of history as we had visited Salzburg, Austria, and seen the places where this family lived. The same mountains that once reminded the von Trapps of Austria now cradle a uniquely American landmark: one built on courage, reinvention, and the enduring harmony of family.

New Hampshire

We took the Kancamagus Highway in **New Hampshire**, a breath-taking 34-mile drive through the White Mountains. No gas stations. No restaurants. Just nature. At a scenic overlook, Natalie, the artist, said, "God took a giant paintbrush to this place." Evelyn, the scientist, chimed in: "Actually, it's the disappearance of green chlorophyll that reveals the brilliant colors that were always there." Science and art go hand in hand on this journey.

Maine

Acadia National Park delivered a grand finale—dramatic cliffs and deep blue ocean.

We left New England full of gratitude for the color, the crisp air, and the reminder that change, though fleeting, can be gloriously beautiful.

SMART TIP: To catch the peak of New England's foliage, plan your trip for mid-September through mid-October, but know that timing varies by state and elevation. The best time to avoid crowds is weekdays and early mornings; therefore, book accommodations well in advance. And don't just stay on main highways: the most magical colors often appear along back roads, small towns, and scenic byways.

Cumberland Island:
Wild Horses and JFK Jr.

"You've got to see the horses," people told us again and again. We hesitated and asked, "Why go all that way to see wild horses?" But we were wrong. Cumberland Island is so much more. It's not just about the horses, it's about mystery, beauty, and a deep sense of history that lingers under the Spanish moss.

Cumberland Island, the largest and southernmost of **Georgia**'s barrier islands, feels like a world apart. Only 300 visitors a day are allowed to board the ferry from St. Mary's. Once on the island, you won't find snack bars or souvenir shops, just untouched nature and timeworn stories. There's one ferry in and one ferry out. Miss it, and you'll have an overnight stay you didn't plan.

A Land of Many Layers

Long before tourists, Cumberland belonged to the Timucua, an influential group of 35 indigenous chiefdoms in North **Florida** and South **Georgia**. Each had its territory and dialect, forming the most significant native presence when the Spanish, and later the British, arrived.

In 1736, General James Oglethorpe established Fort St. Andrews on the island as part of his vision for the new colony of **Georgia**. He imagined it was settled by both "worthy poor" and rehabilitated prisoners as an early social experiment in colonization.

Southern Grandeur and Gilded Dreams

A van tour, the only motorized option, can take you to the island's northern end, where you'll find the ruins of Dungeness. Built first by Catherine Greene (widow of Revolutionary War hero General Nathanael Greene), the home was constructed from tabby, a unique material made by mixing burned oyster shells with sand, ash, and water.

Later, the Carnegie family, among the wealthiest of the Gilded Age, built their own opulent Dungeness on the same site. Although it burned down in 1959, the ruins remain, offering visitors a glimpse into an era of extravagant living.

Elsewhere, the Carnegies built Plum Orchard, a mansion adorned with French doors, expansive terraces, and elegant finishes. It remains intact and can be toured, if you're up for a 7-mile walk or bike ride.

A Secret Wedding and Storied Past

Cumberland was never short on drama. On September 21, 1996, John F. Kennedy Jr. and Carolyn Bessette were married in secret at the island's tiny First African Baptist Church. With no electricity, the ceremony was held by candlelight as the sun slipped below the horizon.

Nature in Its Rawest Form

If you're a nature lover, you're in for a treat and a challenge. The island teems with wildlife: armadillos, alligators, turkeys, shorebirds, and yes—those iconic wild horses. But be prepared: wear sturdy shoes, long pants, and bring plenty of bug spray. There are no paved roads and few conveniences. You take the 4.5-mile hike through the forest and marsh.

The horses, numbering around 150–170, are descendants of animals largely brought over by the British in the 18th century, despite the enduring myth that the Spanish introduced them. Like their cousins on Chincoteague and Assateague, off the coast of **Virginia and Maryland,** they roam free, untamed and iconic. Some question their environmental impact, but the National Park Service manages them as part of the island's living legacy.

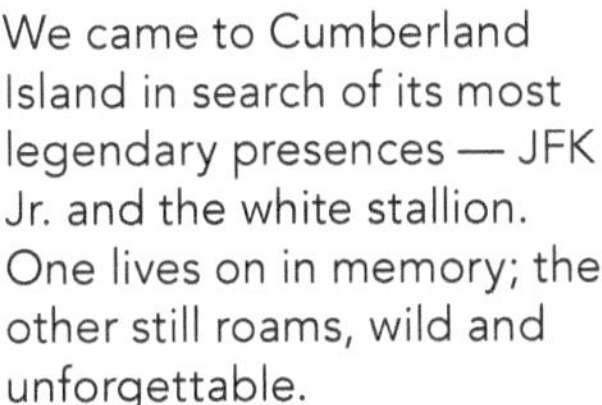

We came to Cumberland Island in search of its most legendary presences — JFK Jr. and the white stallion. One lives on in memory; the other still roams, wild and unforgettable.

Today's Cumberland: Layers of Legacy

What remains in Cumberland today is a mix of old lineages, descendants of enslaved people, former aristocrats, naturalists, and storytellers.

And then there's Carol Ruckdeschel, often called "the wildest woman in America." Living in a ramshackle cabin, she's known for eating roadkill, wrestling alligators, and fiercely defending sea turtles. Her deep understanding of the island's ecology and relentless advocacy have made her a conservation legend.

SMART TIP: Cumberland Island is beautiful, but it's no casual walk. Most visitors walk 4–7 miles on trails of sand, roots, and loose gravel. The National Park Service explicitly warns not to wear flip-flops or open-toe shoes; wear walking shoes. You can take the Lands and Legacy Van Tour or rent a bike.

Lake Tahoe: Diamond of the Sierra Nevada

(Evelyn, Natalie, and Sharlene, the oldest sister)

Just say the words *Lake Tahoe*, and friends light up with excitement. This dazzling gem, straddling **California** and **Nevada**, shimmers like a diamond at sunrise. For us, the perfect reason to visit came when Evelyn's grandson Keenan announced his wedding on the banks of Lake Tahoe.

First Glimpse

Flying into Reno, **Nevada**, we caught a glimpse of the lake among towering mountains. After a meal at the historic Wild River Grille, Sharlene's husband, Ken, took the wheel, and we weren't eager to tackle the curving mountain roads as **Florida** natives.

On the Lake

Lake Tahoe is a blend of crystal-clear waters, mountain peaks, and the warmth of small-town life.

We stayed at Mourelatos Lakeside Resort, a charming lodge with windows framing the lake. Initially built in 1942 and rebuilt after a 1994 fire, it's a modern building with an old-fashioned pulley elevator, open on the sides and trembling with every floor. Riding it felt like a blend of history and a carnival ride, but we braved it, just once.

California: Here We Come

Breakfast at Rosie's Café in Tahoe City started our explorations. A nostalgic diner filled with antique skis, sleds, and Western gear, Rosie's has been a community hub for over 40 years.

From there, we followed the **California** shoreline to Emerald Bay, one of the most photographed spots in the Sierra Nevada. Waterfalls tumbled, and Vikingsholm Castle stood proudly on the shore. A gondola ride at Heavenly Village tempted us, but biting winds sent us back toward Tahoe City.

Penny Bear in Tahoe City

As we strolled along the quaint sidewalks of Tahoe City, we stumbled upon a whimsical surprise: a 12-foot bear sculpture covered in 200,000 pennies, each one catching the light like shimmering fur. Nearby, her coppery cubs gleamed proudly, and just across the street, a wooden bear stood on tiptoe, peering into a second-story window as if checking in on the neighbors.

Rising over 12 feet at Lake Tahoe, Penny Bear—crafted from nearly 200,000 pennies—stands as a monumental work of art. A close-up reveals the intricate detail of each coin, turning small change into something extraordinary.

The Nevada Side

Crossing into **Nevada**, the scenery shifted. Casinos sparkled among the trees, a contrast to the lake's natural beauty. Kayakers paddled in icy water, and a few daring swimmers splashed about.

Incline Village drew us next, famous for sky-high real estate prices. We went searching for traces of the beloved TV series *Bonanza*. The Ponderosa Ranch is now closed, but we laughed over a restaurant menu as we ate a "Hoss Burger" and "Bonanza Burger."

To the Business at Hand: The Wedding

The highlight, of course, was Keenan and Holly's wedding at King's Beach. We, the **Florida** Kellys, had packed snow coats, but they weren't needed. The day was bright, calm, and warm. The lake mirrored the peaks in polished perfection, a breathtaking backdrop for vows of love.

SMART TIP: To enjoy the full beauty of Lake Tahoe, plan a day to drive or cycle around the entire lake. The **Nevada** side is often less crowded and more budget-friendly, yet just as stunning. Summer is perfect for cycling, but start early to beat traffic and secure parking at popular viewpoints.

St. Louis Arch and the Golden Gate Bridge: Bridging a Nation

There are countless American landmarks, but few embody the nation's bold spirit of exploration and innovation like the Gateway Arch in St. Louis and the Golden Gate Bridge in San Francisco. Though separated by geography, time, and architectural style, these two marvels tell one sweeping American story: our national push westward, the courage to chase the horizon, and the belief that the impossible can be built.

The Gateway to the West

From our hotel window in St. Louis, we gaze out at a towering, stainless-steel arch rising from the banks of the Mississippi River. As our eyes trace its perfect curve, we marvel at this engineering masterpiece. Completed in 1965, the Gateway Arch soars 630 feet, taller than both the Statue of Liberty and the Washington Monument.

It was here that America's westward expansion took shape. The Arch stands as a symbolic doorway to the lands beyond—the very lands that fueled the idea of Manifest Destiny, the belief that the nation was meant to span from coast to coast.

Its creation was not without risk. Workers high above the river welded triangular steel sections, curving ever closer until they met at the exact center, completing the vision.

Why an arch? It was built as a tribute to the pioneers who ventured West and a memorial to the men and women who left comfort and familiarity behind to embrace the unknown.

We took the tram to the top, feeling both excitement and a twinge of anxiety as the small car crept through the arch's inner skeleton. From the viewing platform, we looked out over the mighty Mississippi and the vast land stretching westward to the horizon. This was the "Gateway to the West," the symbolic threshold of America's Manifest Destiny.

At the foot of the Arch, inside its small museum, Natalie noticed an enormous footprint embedded in the floor. It belonged to Robert Wadlow, the tallest man ever recorded at 8'11". True to her inquisitive nature, she slipped her own foot inside the outline. Onlookers laughed as Robert's footprint completely swallowed hers, and soon a line formed as others compared their feet to his. Wadlow, who lived in the St. Louis area, remains a striking symbol of the extraordinary extremes of human scale and possibility.

The Bridge to the Pacific

Decades before the Arch was built, but decades after pioneers first pushed past St. Louis, another frontier waited: the Pacific Coast. And at its edge rose the Golden Gate Bridge.

While staying in Oakland, we watched the bridge reveal itself through the fog, locally known as "Karl the Fog," a name from the viral Twitter account @KarlTheFog. As the fog drifted, the top of the rust-red towers emerged.

That this bridge exists at all is astonishing. Built during the Great Depression, the Golden Gate Bridge seemed as impossible as crossing the western plains seemed to early settlers. Yet hundreds came, willing to take on the unthinkable task: building a bridge across San Francisco Bay, one of the most treacherous waterways in the United States. Workers balanced on wind-whipped beams high above the currents of the Golden Gate Strait. Eleven never made it home; nineteen survived dramatic falls by landing in a pioneering safety net and became known as the "Halfway to Hell Club."

Driving across the bridge, we felt its symbolism: a link not only between San Francisco and Marin County, but between daring and accomplishment. Just like the Arch, the Golden Gate is a testament to frontier spirit, this time, the final frontier of the continental United States.

SMART TIP: St. Louis Arch: Check the weather. Clear days offer the best views of the Mississippi River and the cityscape. Foggy or rainy days may limit visibility. The tram and observation platform are small, so be prepared for a snug ride.

San Francisco Golden Gate Bridge: Morning fog gives that iconic, mysterious glow (thanks, Karl), but late afternoon and sunset offer warmer light, clearer views, and the best photos. If you plan to walk the bridge, bring layers; the winds are strong.

Let's Go to the Beach: Memories and Coastlines

Nothing lifts the spirit quite like loading the family into the car—cooler packed, towels in a heap, sunscreen already smeared into someone's hair—and heading for the beach. For generations, shorelines have been where memories are made: first swims, "epic" sandcastles, sunburned noses, picnic mishaps, and long sunset walks that stay with you forever.

What many Americans don't realize is just how incredible—and wildly different—our beaches truly are. Australia may have the Great Barrier Reef, and Greece may shimmer along the Mediterranean, but the USA? We have thousands of miles of coastline, each with its own personality and charm.

Unique Experiences Across the Regions

Let's take a quick tour of America's coastline. This is not a comprehensive guide, but a glimpse at some of our favorite beaches and what makes each region special.

East Coast

Driving the length of U.S. Route 1 feels like flipping through America's coastal scrapbook—each mile a new page, from the misty lighthouses of **Maine** all the way down to the pastel cottages at the road's final stop in Key West, **Florida**.

Bar Harbor, **Maine**: A must-visit for photographers and nature lovers. Sand Beach is nestled between rugged granite cliffs and pine forests, offering striking scenery rather than warm swimming. Bar Harbor sits right on the edge of Acadia National Park, with miles of hiking and biking trails with breathtaking ocean views.

Jekyll Island, **Georgia**: On Jekyll Island, Natalie and Evelyn wandered Driftwood Beach, weaving between ghostly, sculpted branches that lined the shoreline. They joked that Mother Nature sometimes outdoes even Michelangelo.

Natalie snapped a hundred photos that day, yet not a single one captured the quiet, meditative beauty of their walk.

Beautiful Driftwood Beach, Jekyll Island, Georgia

Gulf Coast

If you're a shell collector, **Florida**'s Suncoast is paradise.

Sanibel Island, **Florida**: Sanibel Island curves into the Gulf like a scoop, catching shells brought north by Caribbean currents. Conchs, whelks, scallops, you name it. At the Bailey-Matthews National Shell Museum, there is a 16-inch whelk and a 2-foot horse conch.

Tips for Finding Huge Shells:

- Go after storms or strong cold fronts
- Look at low tide, ideally at dawn
- Scan the high-tide wrack line
- Bring a shell bag and water shoes—they're sharp!

A Detour to Pensacola Beach: **Florida** alone boasts 909 miles of public beachfront, from untouched state parks to lively boardwalks.

After a morning of powder-soft sand and turquoise water at Pensacola Beach, Natalie and Evelyn made a detour to Fort Pickens, the historic brick fort that once imprisoned Apache leader Geronimo—and, much to their surprise, Natalie's great-grandfather, who was held there during the Civil War.

Walking through the echoing corridors, Natalie joked to the guide, "If you're going to be in jail, at least you're imprisoned on the beach!" Even the guide laughed.

West Coast

One of the most beautiful drives in the United States is the Pacific Coast Highway, a ribbon of cliffs and oceans of blue. From the shores of Big Sur down to the sun-drenched beaches of San Diego, it offers breathtaking views at every turn.

Malibu, **California**: When you hear "Malibu," what comes to mind? Rich and famous? Glamorous beachfront parties? Yes, they're there, but there's so much more. Malibu is a showstopper: rugged cliffs, crashing waves, and pink sunsets.

Natalie and Evelyn visited their friend Paul, whose house perches dramatically above the Pacific. From the deck, Natalie scanned the horizon and spotted Catalina Island, faintly outlined. The view was cinematic, majestic, and humbling all at once, a reminder that Malibu isn't just about the lifestyle you see in magazines; it's about nature's magic.

Coronado Beach (near San Diego): Evelyn and Natalie walked along the glimmering shoreline, each step feeling like they were walking on crushed gold. Coronado Beach is famous for the tiny reflective minerals in its sand. It's pure magic under your feet and one of the best beaches in America for building sandcastles.

Towering proudly above this shoreline is the legendary Hotel del Coronado, a grand Victorian mansion. With its iconic red-turreted roof and sweeping verandas, "The Del" has welcomed presidents, movie stars, and dreamers since 1888. Natalie and Evelyn loved wandering its historic hallways, where old-world charm mingles with ocean breezes. Every so often, a Navy helicopter from the nearby base hovered across the sky.

Alaska

Yes, **Alaska** has beaches—and they are breathtaking. On a cruise along the Inside Passage, Evelyn and Natalie stood bundled in jackets on the deck, watching waves lap at rocky shores backed by glaciers and mountains. They still laugh about how they *couldn't* feel their noses afterward, but agreed it was worth every chilly second.

Hawaii

And, of course, no article about American beaches would be complete without a visit to **Hawaii**. Waikiki Beach on Oahu is legendary, with its golden sand beach stretching along the bustling coastline, and the skyline of Honolulu glimmers in the background. Natalie, ever the adventurer, couldn't resist trying her hand at surfing lessons, wobbling and wiping out. Over and over again.

Intracoastal Waterway

Flowing quietly behind the Atlantic and Gulf coasts, the 3,000-mile Intracoastal Waterway is America's secret liquid highway, calm water threading its way past marshes, islands, fishing towns, and hidden pockets of paradise. Engineered initially for shipping and military strategy, it has since softened into something far more exhilarating: a corridor for kayakers, sailors, bird-watchers, and boaters. Natalie and Evelyn spent an afternoon drifting along one of these serene channels, the motor humming softly as dolphins surfaced beside the boat like playful escorts.

SMART TIP: To make the most of your beach adventure, plan around crowds, weather, and tides. Early mornings or weekdays often bring quieter beaches. And remember to check local rules: some beaches limit pets, fires, or certain water activities, so checking ahead ensures a smooth and enjoyable visit.

Our National Parks:
The Best Idea America Had

The beauty of our nation lies in its countless places, each unique and captivating in its own way. We want to honor the National Parks: some world-famous, others less frequented. Read through this list, and you'll understand why Wallace Stegner famously said the parks were "the best idea America ever had."

The Beginning of the Parks

In 1916, President Woodrow Wilson signed the Organic Act, creating the National Park Service. The mission was simple, profound, and revolutionary: preserve America's most breathtaking landscapes and historic wonders and protect them for everyone.

More than a century later, that mission feels even more meaningful. From the Great Smoky Mountains to the Everglades, our parks invite us to slow down, look up, and feel small in the best possible way.

Our 63 National Parks

Below is a brief guide to all 63 national parks, organized by region. Though we haven't visited all of them (yet!), we include articles about seven parks that carry personal meaning for us.

Northeast (1 park)

- Acadia, **Maine** – Windy on the rugged, granite peaks; first sunrise in the USA.

South (12 parks)

- Shenandoah, **Virginia/West Virginia** – Blue Ridge Mountains and hiking.
- New River Gorge, **West Virginia** (reclassified 2020) – Deep gorge, whitewater rafting.
- Mammoth Cave, **Kentucky** – World's longest cave.
- Great Smoky Mountains, **Tennessee/North Carolina** – Rich Appalachian culture; magnificent in fall.
- Congaree, **South Carolina** – Swamp boardwalks and hardwood forests.
- Everglades, **Florida** – Great river of grass and swamp; UNESCO site.
- Biscayne, **Florida** – 95% underwater, coral reefs, near Miami.
- Dry Tortugas, **Florida** – Historic Fort Jefferson, coral reefs.
- Hot Springs, **Arkansas** – Thermal springs, bathhouses.
- Big Bend, **Texas** – Desert, Rio Grande canyons.
- Guadalupe Mountains, **Texas** – Jagged peaks and lots of fossils.
- Virgin Islands, U.S. Virgin Islands – Beaches, coral reefs.

Midwest (5 parks)

- Isle Royale, **Michigan** - Remote islands, moose, and wolves.
- Voyageurs, **Minnesota** – Water-based park, houseboats.
- Gateway Arch, **Missouri** – Iconic stainless-steel arch celebrating westward expansion.
- Cuyahoga Valley, **Ohio** – Waterfalls, historic canal.
- Indiana Dunes, **Indiana** (reclassified 2019) – Lake Michigan dunes.

Intermountain (21 parks)

- Theodore Roosevelt, **North Dakota** – Badlands that shaped a president's vision.
- Badlands, **South Dakota** – Land formations you will not believe.
- Wind Cave, **South Dakota** – Intricate caves and many bison.
- Black Canyon of the Gunnison, **Colorado** – Unusual black cliffs carved by the Colorado River.
- Great Sand Dunes, **Colorado** – Tall dunes framed by snow peaks.
- Mesa Verde, **Colorado** – Cliff dwellings of the ancient Pueblo.
- Rocky Mountains, **Colorado** – Snow-capped peaks, alpine lakes, elk.
- Glacier, **Montana** – Glaciers.
- Yellowstone, **Wyoming/Montana/Idaho** – Geysers, bison, super volcano.
- Grand Canyon, **Arizona** – Canyon carved by the Colorado River.
- Petrified Forest, **Arizona** – Painted petrified logs and desert.
- Saguaro, **Arizona** – Nothing like seeing these giant cacti for the first time.
- Great Basin, **Nevada** – Ancient bristlecones, Lehman Caves.
- Carlsbad, **New Mexico** – Vast caves with a multitude of bats.
- White Sands, **New Mexico** – Dazzling with gypsum moving in the wind.
- Arches, **Utah** – 2000 plus natural sandstone arches.
- Bryce Canyon, **Utah** – World's most extensive hoodoo collection.
- Canyonlands, **Utah** – Colorado River canyons.
- Capitol Reef, **Utah** – Red cliffs mixed with pioneer orchards.
- Zion, **Utah** – Angel's Landing and red sandstone offering breathtaking views.
- Grand Tetons, **Wyoming** – Jagged peaks, Jackson Lake.

Evelyn at Jenny Lake, with the dramatic spires of Grand Teton National Park rising behind her.

Pacific West (16 parks)

- Channel Islands, **California** – Island ecosystems and sea caves.
- Death Valley, **California/Nevada** – Lowest point in North America.
- Joshua Tree National Park, **California** – Desert rock climbing.
- Kings Canyon, **California** – Giant sequoias, deep canyons.
- Lassen Volcanic, **California** – Hydrothermal areas, cinder cone.
- Pinnacles, **California** – Rock spires, California condors.
- Redwood, **California** – World's tallest trees.
- Sequoia, **California** – Home of General Sherman, the world's largest tree.
- Yosemite, **California** – Granite cliffs, waterfalls.
- Crater Lake, **Oregon** – Deepest volcanic lake in the USA.

- Mount Rainier, **Washington** – Established to protect the mountain's glaciers, forests, and unique ecosystems.
- Olympic, **Washington** – Rainforests, coastlines, and glaciered peaks.
- North Cascades, **Washington** – Most glaciers in the lower 48 states.
- Haleakalā, **Hawaii** – Sunrise from above a volcanic summit.
- Hawaii Volcanoes, **Hawaii** – Active lava flows.
- National Park of American Samoa – Coral reefs, tropical rainforest.

Alaska (8 parks)

- Mt. McKinley/Denali – North America's tallest peaks.
- Gates of the Arctic – Wilderness above the Arctic Circle with no roads.
- Glacier Bay – Glaciers and marine life, including whales.
- Katmai – Dramatic glaciers and fjords.
- Kenai Fjords – Coastal fjords, marine wildlife.
- Kobuk Valley – Great sand dunes above the Arctic Circle and lots of caribou.
- Lake Clark – Turquoise lakes, active volcanoes.
- Wrangell-St. Elias – Huge park, larger than the country of Switzerland

---

SMART TIPS: If you're 62 or older, don't miss the America the Beautiful Senior Pass, your ticket to more than 2,000 federal sites, including every national park. It's a one-time purchase that pays for itself in just a few visits.

And for explorers of all ages, pick up the Passport to Your National Parks at any visitor center. Each park visit earns you a stamp in this navy-blue keepsake (similar to our passport), proof of your visit.

Yellowstone: A Year-Round Adventure

Imagine being the first outsider to stumble into Yellowstone. That was John Colter, a rugged pioneer fresh from the Lewis and Clark Expedition. He wandered into a land alive with hissing steam, boiling mud, and geysers that shot water high into the sky. What would you have thought? When he told people what he'd seen, they laughed. "Colter's Hell," they said.

America's First National Park

Colter's hellish visions were real. Yellowstone is a living canvas where history, myth, and geology come together. The Washburn-Langford-Doane Expedition of 1870 brought back journals and sketches that convinced the nation this place needed protection. On March 1, 1872, President Ulysses S. Grant created the world's first National Park.

Yellowstone wears winter well: icy air, geothermal breath, and bison standing strong against a frozen frontier.

Most people think of Yellowstone in summer, but winter flips the script. Crowds vanish. Snow muffles the world. Silence takes over, broken only by distant huffs of bison.

This is the story of a friend's Yellowstone adventure during the winter.

We climbed into a snowcoach, gliding over silent roads to Old Faithful as steam pierced the snowy air. Cross-country skiing along the Firehole River, it felt like we were the first humans there in centuries—just skis, snow, and the hush of the wilderness.

Winter wildlife thrills: bison drifted like shadows across white fields, elk called across frozen valleys, and bald eagles soared overhead, untouchable and majestic. Dog sledding sealed the adventure. A team of eager huskies yipped to go, pulling us through forest trails dusted in snow. Wrapped in wool blankets, bundled in parkas, I felt like a true frontier explorer. John Colter might have envied this.

Yellowstone offers unforgettable experiences, no matter the season.

SMART TIP: Winter in Yellowstone takes planning. Most visitors stay in gateway towns, such as Bozeman, West Yellowstone, and Jackson Hole, because accommodations like Old Faithful Lodge are limited. You get the park almost to yourself.

The Grand Canyon: Trail Blazers, Legends, and Canyon Queens

The Grand Canyon is one of those "ooo-ahh" places. More than five million people visit every year, staring into a chasm so vast that the entire state of **Rhode Island** could disappear inside it. However, even with all the cameras snapping and tour buses arriving, the Canyon keeps its secrets—wild caves no one has mapped, endangered animals tucked into hidden side canyons, and layers of rock that leave even the experts puzzled.

There are so many unknowns about the Grand Canyon that geologists still scratch their heads over the 1.2 billion years that are missing. Adventurers vanish without a trace, like Glen and Bessie Hyde, the newlyweds who set off down the Colorado River in 1928 and were never seen again.

As Natalie stands at the rim of the Grand Canyon, fear gives way to thoughts of the women whose leadership helped shape this place.

But when Evelyn and Natalie stood at the rim, wind tugging at their jackets, the light shifting across the cliffs, they didn't think of mysteries or tragedies. They thought of the women who had walked here before them: women who stood where they stood, felt the same awe, and faced this wilderness with skirts brushing the dust and courage as deep as the gorge itself.

Evelyn leaned on the stone wall of the El Tovar Hotel and joked, "If Ada Fuller could haul water in a corset, surely we can manage a stroll along the rim." Natalie laughed, her eyes scanning the horizon, imagining the Harvey Girls bustling around the hotel in crisp white aprons and the trailblazing women who carved their stories into the Canyon.

Ada Fuller: The Pianist Who Tried Canyon Life

Take Ada Fuller, a gifted pianist from **New York**. In her twenties, she traveled west to visit her aunt in Prescott, **Arizona**, and curiosity drew her to the Canyon. It was a wild, isolated place then, with trails carved more by mules than men. Her guide was William Wallace (W. W.) Bass, a man who loved geology and poetry and carried a violin under his arm. He played by firelight, the notes floating out into the night air. Ada was enchanted by the music, by the man, and perhaps by the Canyon itself.

She married Bass in 1885 and began the hard life of a pioneer woman at the Canyon's edge. Her days were filled with hauling water from the river, scrubbing laundry in icy streams, cooking meals for trail-dusted travelers, and doing it all in heavy skirts that dragged through mud and dust. For a time, she went back to the East Coast. However, the Canyon and Bass called her back.

When tourists arrived by railroad in 1901, Ada watched them fall silent in awe.

The Harvey Girls: Civilizing the Rim

The railroad also brought Fred Harvey's hospitality empire. He filled his dining rooms with young women from the East, Harvey Girls, as they came to be known, who escaped factory jobs in search of something bigger. At the El Tovar Hotel, which opened in 1905, they served elegant meals under glittering chandeliers, even as cowboys and pack mules lingered outside the doors.

Rules governed their lives: no chewing gum, strict curfews, supervised dormitories. But their pay was good, their reputations intact, and their world suddenly filled with adventure. They weren't just servers; they were trailblazers, helping to bring grace and culture to a rugged frontier.

Mary Colter: Architect of the Canyon

Then came Mary Colter, the visionary architect who designed the Hopi House, Lookout Studio, Desert View Watchtower, and Phantom Ranch. Her style honored Native traditions and blended seamlessly with the Canyon's natural rock.

Evelyn and Natalie stepped into the Hopi House and felt as though time had folded: Native art displayed just as it had been for more than a century, the stone walls echoing the spirit of Colter's genius.

Elzada Clover and Lois Jotter: Pioneers on the River

And then there were the women who took to the river itself. In 1938, botanists Elzada Clover and Lois Jotter were told flatly that women couldn't survive rafting the Colorado. They went anyway. Their journals filled with notes on new plant discoveries, they proved the naysayers wrong, completing the journey and etching their names into the Canyon's story.

The Grand Canyon is eternal, humbling, and vast beyond imagination. But if you stand quietly at its edge, you might hear more than the wind in the pines or the rush of the **Colorado** far below. You might hear Ada Fuller's piano drifting out of a saloon, the voices of Harvey Girls bustling in the dining room, Mary Colter's pen sketching a tower against the sky, or Clover and Jotter's laughter echoing off canyon walls.

SMART TIP: Follow in the footsteps of the Canyon's fearless women by joining a ranger-led program. From botany walks to history talks, you'll see how passion and courage still shape this canyon.

From Acadia to Louisiana:
A Tale of Two Worlds

Did you know there's a deep connection between the Cajun people of **Louisiana** and the far-northeast corner of the country, today's state of **Maine**? Evelyn and Natalie didn't either, at least not until they stood on the granite cliffs of Acadia National Park one year, bundled in jackets, and later found themselves floating down a Louisiana bayou, listening to accordions and dodging mosquitoes the size of hummingbirds.

This is a story that connects two very different worlds, just as travel so often does.

The Acadians: A Journey of Courage and Heartbreak

In the 1600s, French settlers, Acadians, made their home in the harsh, beautiful landscape of the Northeast. They were tough people who coaxed crops out of rocky soil and built ingenious dikes to hold back the sea. But the French and Indian War turned their lives upside down. When the British won, they feared the Acadians might support France.

Their solution? Expel them.

Families were separated, homes burned, and thousands were forced into exile. Some made a long, grueling journey to an entirely different world: **Louisiana**.

From Granite Cliffs to Swamps

Imagine the shock. One day you're breathing in crisp Atlantic air, and the next you're stepping into a landscape buzzing with insects and filled with creatures you'd only heard rumors about. A traveler once told Evelyn, "The first time I saw an alligator, I thought it was a log until it blinked."

The Acadians had to adapt quickly. They traded lobsters for gumbo, icy winters for steamy summers, and granite coasts for cypress swamps. Out of hardship grew Cajun culture: warm, energetic, and vibrant.

"The Story of Evangeline"

If you grew up reading American literature, you probably remember Henry Wadsworth Longfellow's poem "Evangeline." Written in 1847, it tells the story of a young Acadian woman who spends her life searching for her lost love, Gabriel, after they're separated during the expulsion. At last, she finds him, but only to watch him die in her arms. Sad? Yes. Overly romantic? Definitely. But it put the Acadian tragedy into the American imagination and made sure it wasn't forgotten.

Cajuns Today

Fast forward to today, and Cajun culture is one of the most colorful in America. Instead of quiet Bar Harbor cafés, you'll find lively kitchens filled with the smells of gumbo and jambalaya. Music spills out of dance halls, fiddles, and accordions, keeping everyone on their feet. People gather under sprawling live oak trees, their branches draped with Spanish moss, and tell stories that stretch into the night.

Even their college sports team celebrates the legacy: the Ragin' Cajuns of the University of Louisiana at Lafayette. The name says it all: fiery, fun, and full of life.

A Park with a French Name

Acadia National Park is often called the crown jewel of the North Atlantic coast. The moment you stand on Cadillac Mountain, you understand why. This is the first place in the United States to catch the sunrise (October-March). It's not a gentle, postcard sunrise either; it's cold, windy, and the kind of beauty that wakes you up. Granite cliffs tumble toward the sea, waves crash with force, and the spruce trees look like they've been bracing themselves for centuries.

On the north side of the park is Bar Harbor, a town that made us feel welcome. We ducked into a little restaurant where we tried our very first **Maine** lobster roll, hot and buttery. One friend told us he and his wife drove from **Florida** to Bar Harbor just for the lobster rolls. They were not disappointed.

SMART TIP: Visit Acadia to feel the roots. Then head to **Louisiana's** bayous to taste the rebirth of a culture: one people, two worlds, one incredible story.

Badlands National Park: Wild Rocks and Weird Shops

S outh Dakota is full of surprises. One minute, we are riding through a rugged wilderness that feels like another planet, and the next, we are in a bustling, old-fashioned drugstore where tourists line up for free ice water. What fun under those vast, azure skies, two places that couldn't be more opposite, yet together make for one unforgettable adventure. It was a journey that swung from prairie dogs to souvenir hunters, from silence to spectacle.

Badlands: Mars in the Midwest

We rolled across land as flat as a pancake when suddenly the earth dropped away. It was as if we had been transported straight to Mars. All we could manage were gasps of "ohhh" and "ahhh" as striped cliffs and jagged peaks stretched across the horizon.

Evelyn pointed out the sedimentary layers, bands of gray, pink, purple, and gold, formed over millions of years as sediments pressed and hardened into stone. Natalie said with a laugh, "It looks like Neapolitan ice cream to me." That ended the geology lecture, and from then on, the cliffs became frosting swirls, the rocks high-fashion models strutting in their most glamorous attire.

But beauty here is fleeting. Erosion eats away up to an inch per year, and in half a million years, this otherworldly landscape may vanish. No wonder the Lakota people called it *mako sica*, "bad lands." Farming is nearly impossible here, with blistering summers, frigid winters, and stubborn soil. Yet life persists. Bison lumber across the plains, often blocking the road. Bighorn sheep perform daredevil leaps across cliffs. And best of all, hundreds of prairie dogs pop up from burrows, chattering like gossiping neighbors.

The Badlands are also a fossil treasure trove. Once upon a time, saber-toothed cats, three-toed horses, and giant rhino-like brontotheres roamed this land. Hollywood has roamed here, too; the dramatic scenery provided a backdrop for blockbuster movies like *Dances with Wolves.*

Put it all together, and you have a geologist's dream, a movie-maker's stage, and a traveler's wonderland. These "bad lands" are, in truth, amazing.

Wall Drug

After the quiet majesty of the Badlands, we found ourselves on a prairie highway, staring at one hand-painted sign after another: *Wall Drug Store... Free Ice Water... Coffee 5 Cents.* The build-up was relentless. By the time we arrived at the massive "Wall Drug Store – Since 1931" sign, we were hooked.

Wall Drug isn't really a drugstore anymore; it's an institution. In 1931, Ted Hustead opened it, but business was bleak until his wife, Dorothy, suggested they lure in travelers with a simple offer: free ice water. It worked. Located just north of the Badlands, Wall Drug turned into a phenomenon.

Today, it's a two-block carnival of cowboy paraphernalia, Western art, and kitschy souvenirs. You can sip that 5-cent coffee, pose with a jackalope (the mythical jackrabbit with antelope horns), or let the kids loose in the backyard with its animatronic *T. rex* and playground. At the height of summer, 20,000 visitors might pass through in a single day. People-watching is half the entertainment.

Reactions vary. Some dismiss it as a gaudy tourist trap; others embrace its quirky, old-timey charm. Either way, when you've been driving dusty **South Dakota** highways in July, that free ice water tastes pretty sweet.

SMART TIP: Pair the two, the Badlands and Wall Drug, and they go hand in hand. Stay overnight in Wall, in a motel or campground, and you'll be perfectly placed to catch both sunrise and sunset over the Badlands. Then toast the day with coffee that still costs just a nickel.

Olympic National Park: Held by Roots, Shaped by Water

By Evelyn Kelly with Master Photographer John Hile

Photography allows us to slow down and find meaning in the ordinary. It can become a mission, a way of seeing, and even a way of being.

One of the great joys is taking photographs. Our magnificent national parks offer breathtaking natural wonders that draw visitors from around the world and provide countless opportunities to capture moments that stay with us long after the trip ends.

My friend John Hile has photographed two awe-inspiring scenes that have captivated travelers for years: a solitary Sitka spruce clinging to life atop an eroding bluff and a dramatic waterfall hidden in a lush forest. Both are located in Olympic National Park.

Olympic National Park: A Pacific Northwest Treasure

Olympic National Park is among the most visited national parks. Established in 1938 to protect **Washington's** disappearing primeval forests, the park now safeguards one of the largest remaining areas of old-growth forest and temperate rainforest in the lower 48 states.

The Olympic Peninsula has been home to Native American tribes for centuries. The Quinault, whose reservation is nearby, still holds land in the area. In their language, the word *Kalaloch* means "a good place to land." It's a fitting name for a place that continues to inspire wonder and for the seed that once landed there and became the famous Tree of Life.

Kalaloch: **The Tree of Life**

This tree is more than a photo op; it's a miracle of nature. An ancient Sitka spruce appears to defy gravity as it stretches its green branches toward the sky, clinging to life above a hollowed-out coastal bluff with no visible soil beneath it. Beneath the tree is a cave-like gap formed by erosion, which visitors have dubbed the "Tree Root Cave."

Facing the wild, crashing waves of the Pacific Ocean, the Tree of Life, also called the "Runaway Tree," has stood resilient against time and tide. No one knows exactly how old it is or how long it has hung on. Until the internet and blogs brought it to fame, this marvel was relatively unknown. Today, it's a beloved and widely shared symbol of

As dawn finally broke over *Kalaloch* Beach, soft sunbeams lit the Tree of Life, an ancient spruce hanging on against gravity and the crashing Pacific. Photo Credit: John Hile

survival, even boasting its own social media following.

Through the Lens: A Photographer's View

In John's words:

"Olympic National Park's Tree of Life, at *Kalaloch* Beach, is unlike anything I've seen. I arrived before sunrise and noticed another photographer already there. But when the sunrise lacked color, he left. I lingered. About 20 minutes later, faint rays of light began to backlight the upper branches of the tree. The cool coastal air made the sunbeams visible, an extraordinary moment worth the wait. The photo I captured was taken about 45 minutes after the official sunrise."

An Inevitable Goodbye

Sadly, the Tree of Life cannot hold on forever. Gravity pulls, the roots strain, and eventually, it will fall. But for now, it stands. And we can still witness its quiet defiance.

Sol Duc Falls: A Cascading Wonder

Why go to Norway to see waterfalls when you can visit Sol Duc Falls right here in Olympic National Park?

This magnificent waterfall splits into multiple channels, sometimes up to four, before plunging 48 to 50 feet into a narrow, rocky gorge. Surrounded by lush moss and towering trees, Sol Duc Falls is tucked deep within an enchanting old-growth forest.

Even its name is poetic. From the Quileute word meaning "sparkling waters" or "magic waters," Sol Duc Falls lives up to its promise.

SMART TIP: Kalaloch Beach: If you want to see the Tree of Life, visit Kalaloch Beach, just west of the Kalaloch Campground off U.S. 101. The historic Kalaloch Lodge, just south of the tree, makes for a perfect base.

Sol Duc: Enjoy the falls from the designated viewing platforms, and never underestimate how slick the mossy rocks can be. There have been reports of visitors tragically slipping while jumping across moss-covered rocks.

Flying into the Dry Tortugas: Pirates, Plagues, and Prisons

Visiting the Dry Tortugas was at the very top of our travel list. We went in December, a cold day even by **Florida** standards. The park entrance is at the ferry terminal in Key West, but we opted for the faster option: a 70-mile seaplane trip.

The brisk wind whipped up the water, and to board we had to wade several feet from shore. Then came the real challenge: climbing a six-rung ladder with no rails and nothing to hold on to. Evelyn's first instinct? "Nope! I'll wait in the lobby." But the others weren't having it.

With a push from behind (on both sides), she was hoisted into the plane, entirely out of her comfort zone.

From above, the water shifted from deep sapphire to glowing turquoise. Beneath us lay a place so remote that every wave seemed to whisper stories from centuries past.

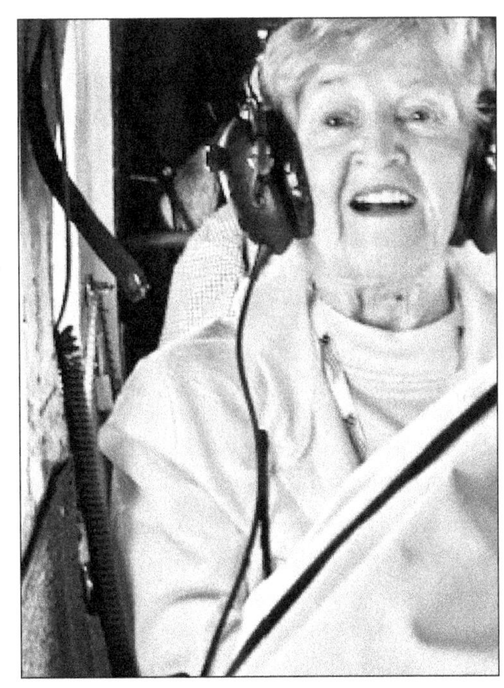

Evelyn is in a seaplane to the Dry Tortugas. She has a panoramic view of turquoise waters and the places where Spanish galleons went down with their cargo of treasures.

1513 – Here Comes the Spanish

Ponce de León dropped anchor here in his search for the Fountain of Youth. He didn't find it. Spanish maps warned sailors in bold letters: DRY Bring your own barrels. The "Tortugas" part came from the hundreds of sea turtles on the island. And so, the Dry Tortugas got their name.

Three Decades– Pirates Arrive

Perfectly positioned near major shipping lanes, the islands became a pirate haven. They plundered turtle eggs, traded turtle meat like currency, and preyed on passing ships. Robert Louis Stevenson's *Treasure Island* could have been inspired here.

Over 200 shipwrecks have occurred in these waters. From the seaplane, you can still spot excavation sites. The most famous wreck, the Nuestra Señora de Atocha (1622), carried gold, silver, and emeralds. Treasure hunter Mel Fisher recovered much of it in the 1980s, igniting a new wave of gold fever.

Fort Jefferson – America's Island Fortress

In 1846, the USA began building a massive coastal defense: 16 million bricks were shipped to these remote islands. Fort Jefferson was never finished, never attacked, but it stood as a symbol of America's ambition.

Inside, the fort became a prison for Union military offenders and Confederate sympathizers. Among them: Dr. Samuel Mudd, who treated John Wilkes Booth's broken leg. Mudd claimed he didn't know Lincoln had been shot, a story the military didn't buy.

The Plague of "Yellow Jack"

Yellow fever, known as "Yellow Jack", was the fort's most feared enemy. In August 1867, an outbreak resulted in the deaths of many, including senior officers. Dr. Mudd treated the sick tirelessly, earning a pardon from President Andrew Johnson.

Today's Visitors

Some come to snorkel or swim in the crystal waters. Others arrive for world-class birdwatching. But for all, the island's dramatic history is never far away; it's a journey to the edge of the world, just 70 miles from Key West.

SMART TIP: From Key West, you can reach the park by ferry or seaplane. In June, July, or August, the ferry's three-hour ride is manageable. The rest of the year? Bring motion sickness medication if you choose that route. Our recommendation: take the seaplane—it's faster, smoother, and the view alone is worth the trip.

Everglades National Park: Swamp Drama

We climb aboard the tram, ready for our next adventure in America's National Parks: the **Florida** Everglades. The sky above us stretches wide and endless, classic **Florida** big sky, already blushing with the soft gold of early morning. Natalie leans over to Evelyn, "Remember when we did the airboat ride? This time it's going to be up close and personal."

Sawgrass for Miles and Miles

The first thing that greets us is an ocean of sawgrass, stretching farther than the imagination. At first glance, it seems plain, but don't be fooled, this is no wallflower. Those sharp blades can slice like a saw, and hidden among them are over a hundred species of native grasses. Cypress trees lift their knees out of the water, while mangroves tangle themselves in complicated embraces.

Birds of a Feather

If birds were party guests, the Everglades would be hosting a grand ball. Egrets are the most social of the bunch, flitting everywhere in their snowy gowns. A roseate spoonbill swishes past, dressed in pink. Wood storks play the part of the tall, elegant guests. And the anhingas, they're the divas, stretching their wings dramatically on poles as if demanding we applaud.

Animals Too

But the Everglades is not all elegance; it has a wild side. Suddenly, the air fills with an unmistakable smell. "Something died," Natalie mutters. And she's right. We catch sight of an alligator eating a python, the ultimate swamp showdown. This gator caught the invasive python when it wasn't looking, held it underwater, and then emerged to start this feast. The gator wins, of course, and then settles in for a meal that could keep it content for months.

And that's only one chapter of this animal love story. Where else can you find alligators and crocodiles living side by side? (It's like Romeo and Juliet, but with more teeth.) Add in

Face-to-face with the king of the Everglades. Survival plays out in real time as an alligator triumphs over a python.

manatees, Florida panthers, black bears, otters, and the occasional marsh rabbit, and you've got quite the cast of characters.

The Glades' Greatest Champion

For centuries, people dismissed the Everglades as useless swamp—something to drain, tame, and build over. But then along came Marjory Stoneman Douglas (1890–1998), journalist, activist, and unlikely matchmaker. She fell head over heels for the Everglades and spent her life convincing others to do the same.

Her book, *The Everglades: River of Grass* (1947), opened with the unforgettable line: *"There are no other Everglades in the world."* She wrote not with the cold eye of a scientist, but with the ardor of someone describing a beloved. Thanks to her, the world finally began to see the Glades not as wasted land, but as a living river worth saving.

The Park

Later that same year, President Harry S. Truman sealed the deal, formally dedicating 1.5 million acres as Everglades National Park. It became the first national park not defined by mountains or canyons but by a subtropical wilderness.

SMART TIP: The Everglades has three main entrances: Shark Valley, Ernest F. Coe (Homestead), and Gulf Coast (Everglades City), each offering a different experience. Take a tram through Shark Valley for alligator sightings and wildlife galore, or hop on an airboat near the Gulf Coast for a thrilling glide across the sawgrass. No matter where you start, pack mosquito repellent, a hat, and light protective clothing; you will be glad you did!

PART 2

History You Can Touch

Writing the story of America isn't confined to books; it's etched into the very ground we walk on. Follow Boston's cobblestone streets where revolution took root, and gaze up at the granite faces of Mount Rushmore that continue to inspire us. Stroll through Native American homelands, and stand on Civil War battlefields where the echoes of a divided nation still linger. Visit the places where our space explorers once stood and reached for the stars. Every step reminds us that history isn't merely studied; it's experienced and honored.

Boston Freedom Trail: Fenway, the Boston Terrier Who Guides Us

(Sometimes it is good to get a perspective of significant historical events through the eyes of a dedicated animal. Fennie is a fictional Boston Terrier who will help us understand the Freedom Trail.)

Hi there! I'm Fenway the Boston Terrier—but you can call me Fennie. I've been hired (paid in treats, of course) to take Evelyn and Natalie on a walk along Boston's famous Freedom Trail.

They picked me because of my dashing black-and-white coat; I look like a gentleman in a tuxedo. But what they don't know is that under this formal attire, I'm a total clown. I plan to entertain them the whole way. They come from a faraway, exotic land called **Florida**, but with today's Boston heat wave, they should feel right at home.

A Real Yankee Doodle Doggie

I'm not just any pup. I'm one of the few truly American breeds, born right here in Boston in the late 19th century. My ancestor, a dog named Judge, was the result of an English Bulldog and a now-extinct White English Terrier. I'm a national treasure.

Evelyn and Natalie are ready, so grab my leash, pack some water (it's a scorcher), and let's follow that 2.5-mile red brick line.

While on Boston's Freedom Trail, Natalie shows off a stuffed Boston Terrier. This breed is one of the few dogs developed entirely in the United States, originating in Boston, Massachusetts, in the late 1800s.

Our Stops on the Freedom Trail:

1. Boston Commons

Our first stop! It's the oldest public park in the United States, here since 1634, that's over 1,000 years in dog years (okay, maybe not quite that long)! It's been a pasture, British military camp, and even a spot for public hangings, including suspected pirates and witches. It was a space used for public gatherings by free-speech advocates such as Frederick Douglass, Martin Luther King, and Pope John Paul II. Today, it's a place to play. I led us to the Frog Pond. It has no frogs—just statues—and on hot days like this, it's a splash zone. In winter, it turns into an ice rink (brrr!).

2. Massachusetts State House

Check out that shiny gold dome! I bark respectfully at the oldest state capitol in the country. This is where humans make big decisions, including laws about dog ownership. Important stuff.

3. Park Street Church

The church has an elegant spire and lovely chimes that ring twice a day. This corner used to be called Brimstone Corner, a hotbed of fiery sermons. It's a reminder that even small barks (like mine) can make a difference.

4. Granary Burying Ground

Here lie Paul Revere, John Hancock, and Samuel Adams. No digging up bones, please, I'm on my best behavior.

5. King's Chapel & Burying Ground

Natalie and Evelyn went on a ghost tour here at the oldest cemetery in Boston. It rained. No ghosts. I suspect they were hiding from the weather.

6. Boston Latin School Site / Ben Franklin Statue

Ben didn't have a dog (poor guy), but he does have a lovely statue. I left my mark, a sniff, not what you're thinking.

7. Old Corner Bookstore

Now a burrito joint (tortillas over tomes?). But once, great writers like Longfellow hung out here. I'd have loved to listen in.

8. Old South Meeting House

The Boston Tea Party started here. Me? I'll take chicken broth over tea any day.

9. Old State House

Humans shouted about taxes. I barked at a pro-British pigeon.

10. Boston Massacre Site

A solemn and sacred place. I stayed silent, paws respectfully still.

11. Faneuil Hall

Heaven for a food-motivated pup like me! Crackers! Pretzels! Natalie bought a plush Boston Terrier. Evelyn scored a "Dog Mama" sweatshirt. Very accurate.

12. Paul Revere House

A real American hero lived here. He rode a horse—I prefer sidewalks.

13. Old North Church

"One if by land, two if by sea." And one bark from me if there's a squirrel.

14. Copp's Hill Burying Ground

We climbed a hill to look out over the harbor. I needed a snack after that workout.

15. USS Constitution

This ship is BIG. I wasn't allowed aboard, but I guarded the dock like a good sailor.

16. Bunker Hill Monument

Final stop! "Don't fire till you see the whites of their eyes!" They yelled when ready to go to war with the British. Evelyn and Natalie loved my walking tour. I got a huge tip, a Greenie! Best. Day. Ever.

SMART TIP (FROM FENNIE): Don't miss the Freedom Trail Walk. All the guides are excellent, even the two-legged ones. Wear comfortable shoes and bring water, especially in summer heat, because the 2.5-mile trail has a lot of ground to cover. But hey, if you're lucky, maybe a Boston Terrier like me will show you around.

The Statue of Liberty: A Reminder of the Price of Freedom

Riding into New York Harbor, our eyes land on the Statue of Liberty for the first time. Sure, we have seen her in pictures, on television, and have read Emma Lazarus' poem: "Give me your tired, your poor masses yearning to be free," but this is not the same. As we stood there, we realized this was not just a **New York** icon but a reminder of freedom, justice, and compassion.

The story of America is written in blood, sweat, and tears. We ask ourselves: how did people find the courage to leave the comfort of their homelands and make such a perilous journey across the ocean? Yet the harsh conditions in their countries gave rise to one burning hope: the dream of a land where they could be free.

The Colonial Period: Mountaineers and Southerners

Our own families came in the Colonial era. Some arrived as indentured servants, working for 4 to 7 years before gaining their freedom; others sold all they owned to pay for the voyage. After landing in Charleston, the Bell family (English and Scots-Irish) moved west into the mountains of what is now Tennessee. The Kelly family (also Scots-Irish) headed south. Passage from Europe cost $1,200–$2,400 in today's money, a fortune at the time (most arrived indentured).

Mid-1800s: The Great Migration

By 1845, Irish peasants relied almost entirely on potatoes for food. That year, a water mold caused crops to rot. Combined with an exploitive British system, the famine from 1845 to 1852 killed more than a million people and drove over two million to emigrate.

Most sold everything to afford passage in steerage, the lowest deck, near the engines and cargo. Conditions were appalling: no privacy, poor ventilation, damp air reeking of filth. Steamships crammed in 1,000–2,000 passengers like cargo. It is hard to fathom what they endured.

Late 1800s to Early 1900s: The Ellis Island Era

During this era, Italians, Jews, Greeks, and countless others made the 7–14-day voyage to New York in steerage. In the peak year of 1907, more than 90% of immigrants arrived this way.

Ellis Island awaited them. Immigrants underwent health checks, skill assessments, and tests of whether they could support themselves. We visited Ellis Island with a friend whose father had immigrated from Hungary. In the great registry hall, she searched the database and found his name, along with his journey and destination to **Michigan**.

The First View of the Statue of Liberty

Imagine what it was like for those weary travelers, packed into rocking ships for weeks on end. For those fleeing famine, persecution, or poverty, Lady Liberty was not just a statue; it was a promise of hope, freedom, and the chance at a better life. Many immigrants cheered, wept, or prayed upon seeing her.

The first glimpse of Lady Liberty is emotional. For generations who crossed oceans with little more than hope, she stood as a promise: freedom, justice, compassion, and the chance to begin again.

The 1920s and Beyond

By the 1920s, strict quotas drastically reduced immigration. By the 1930s, the price of passage had risen to $1,400–$2,100 in today's money. Even the cheapest steerage ticket required months or years of savings. Most arrived with little more than a small suitcase of clothes and the determination to start anew.

SMART TIP: Book your ferry early, especially in the summer, and visit both Liberty Island and Ellis Island. Start at the Statue of Liberty Museum. Then visit the Great Hall at Ellis Island. Grab a Junior Ranger booklet if you have little ones, or trace your own family's journey. After your visit, stop by Battery Park or hop on the free Staten Island Ferry for more stunning views of the harbor and skyline of Manhattan.

Mount Rushmore: America's History in Stone Faces

It is a very hot day in **South Dakota** when we see it for the first time: Mount Rushmore, with its faces carved in granite. We are in awe. As we walked towards the monument, we were met by a wide trail lined with flags of every state on both sides. Four presidents look over the Black Hills. But it is more than faces. It is more than just a tourist attraction. It is little children waving flags and rangers telling the story of a nation born of the ideals of the Enlightenment, tested by war, and transformed into a single, powerful country. Not always perfect, but committed to the belief that all are created equal.

Let's Bring Visitors to South Dakota

Where did this marvelous engineering feat originate? A **South Dakota** historian, Doane Robinson, believed that more people should see the state's spectacular sights. He imagined the heroes of the West, like Buffalo Bill, but sculptor

Four presidents. One nation. A corridor of flags leading to the granite legacy of Mount Rushmore National Memorial —symbols of America's enduring promise.

Gutzon Borglum had a vision of carving the faces of four presidents who had shaped the USA.

In 1927, dynamite, jackhammers, and precision drilling were used to sculpt the 60-foot-high faces. It took 14 years.

Choosing the Four Presidents

Each one was chosen because they represented some role or ideal in shaping the country.

- George Washington- Founding father, representing the birth of the USA.
- Thomas Jefferson- Author of the Declaration of Independence and advocate of growth and expansion.
- Abraham Lincoln - Determined to preserve the Union, ended slavery.
- Theodore Roosevelt - Champion of progress, national parks, global influence.

These four tell part of the story- but not all.

What a Trip to South Dakota Means

While in a hair salon, the hairstylist told us how her husband and teenage son had taken the trip of a lifetime, their first road trip to Mount Rushmore. It was so meaningful and exciting, and they came home so enthusiastic about seeing this great monument. For them and many Americans, it is a patriotic privilege, full of awe and pride in our nation.

Some may disagree with the location on the lands of Native People. That is why we were so pleased to combine the two: Mount Rushmore and Crazy Horse Memorial are only a few miles apart. We see both of them as important. We view them as a part of the past and also America's future.

SMART TIP: Visit Mount Rushmore in the morning as the sun rises on the stone granite, revealing every chiseled detail and beating the crowds. Then, take a scenic drive to the Crazy Horse Memorial. Spend time in the museum and cultural center, where you can watch the ongoing carving progress and learn about Lakota history. Go back later to Mount Rushmore for an entirely different experience of a laser show at night.

Honoring the
First Americans

By Evelyn

Cherokees in the Mountains of North Carolina

From the time I was a young girl, I've been drawn to the history of Native Americans, those who lived on this land long before it was called America. My grandfather, Papa Bell, was born on the Cherokee reservation in the **North Carolina** mountains. According to family stories, his mother was of Cherokee descent and his father of Scots-Irish heritage. They named their son George Washington Bell, a tribute to their devotion to the ideals of the American Revolution. He was born on June 20, 1880.

But the spark he ignited in me lives on. It fuels our continuing love affair with the story of America, especially the story of its first people.

Where the Trail of Tears Began

We are in Savannah, **Tennessee**, a quiet town by the Tennessee River. But in 1838, it was a tragic waypoint for the Cherokee, Choctaw, and other Native peoples who were forced westward to Indian Territory, now **Oklahoma**. The Indian Removal Act of 1830 had promised land west of the **Mississippi** in exchange for their Southeastern homelands, along with financial assistance and protection. Those promises, however, were rarely kept.

Here, at the major departure point on the water route of the Trail of Tears, we walk through memorials and museums that share stories of sorrow and strength. The air feels heavy with memory. These people weren't simply relocated; they were displaced, torn from sacred homelands. They were promised a future where they could preserve their tribal ways, but the cost was devastating.

Eastern Band of the Cherokees

Not all Cherokees left. Three groups remained in the East:
- Some hid in the remote coves of the Great Smoky Mountains.
- A few were granted land or received exemptions.
- Others escaped from removal parties and returned to their homeland.

These determined survivors became what we now know as the Eastern Band of Cherokee Indians. My grandfather was born decades after the removal, and even his father, born in 1850, grew up in its long shadow.

Today, as we drive through the village of Cherokee, **North Carolina,** we feel the heartbeat of a people who refused to disappear. Their resilience is visible everywhere in the language, the crafts, and the stories. It is a vibrant symbol of cultural survival and pride.

To South Dakota: Honoring a Warrior

It's a blistering day in **South Dakota** as we approach a monumental figure rising from the granite of the Black Hills. This is the Crazy Horse Memorial, unfinished, unfunded by the government, but unforgettable.

Crazy Horse was never photographed and remained a mystery even in his own time. Now, his likeness, carved in stone, gazes across the sacred hills of his ancestors. We walked through the museum, surrounded by beadwork, drums, photos, and powerful exhibits that honor the stories of hundreds of Native nations. We agreed that it's one of the best Indigenous museums in the USA.

Crazy Horse, born around 1840-42, lived for the freedom and dignity of his people. At the Battle of the Little Bighorn, he led the fight that defeated General Custer's forces, securing his place in legend. But that victory

Carved into the Black Hills, the Crazy Horse Memorial is a powerful tribute to courage, cultural pride, and the enduring spirit of Native nations.

also sealed his fate; he was betrayed and fatally stabbed at Fort Robinson. Yet his spirit endures, both in the mountain and in the hearts of those who remember him.

Let Us Honor the First Americans

The First Americans were the original stewards of this land. Their deep spiritual connection to the earth, along with their wisdom, resilience, and cultural richness, has profoundly shaped our nation. From the proud tribes of the West, to the Wampanoag who welcomed the Pilgrims, to the indomitable Seminoles of **Florida**, who never surrendered, let us remember and honor the enduring legacy of all Indigenous peoples.

SMART TIP: Visit Cherokee, **North Carolina**; explore the Trail of Tears historic site in Savannah, **Tennessee**; and stand in awe before the Crazy Horse Memorial in **South Dakota**. Walk in the footsteps of those who came before, not just to see monuments, but to understand meaning. These journeys are not only about travel. They are about the soul of America.

Winter with Lewis and Clark at Fort Clatsop

(This story is told from the point of view of Private Joe,
a member of the Corps of Discovery)

When President Jefferson purchased that vast stretch of land from France, people back home barely understood its significance: wild rivers, endless trees, native tribes, and maybe a water path to the Pacific.

I, Joe, was a poor boy from **Kentucky** who'd never seen the ocean. But when I heard there was an expedition headed west to carve out the future of America, I signed up without blinking.

We called ourselves the Corps of Discovery. That sounded mighty fine at the start, like we'd be adventurers, maybe even heroes. We left in 1804. We didn't know then how long we'd be gone or how much it would change us.

We walked, paddled, and hauled ourselves across nearly 8,000 miles of untamed wilderness, farther than any American expedition had ever gone. We crossed roaring rivers, climbed mountains where snow swallowed our boots, and slept on frozen ground. There were no maps. No doctors. No roads. Just grit and each other.

And finally, one gray day, we reached the edge of the Pacific Ocean. I cried when I saw it. Salt wind on my face, the roaring waves. I'd never imagined anything so big. But joy faded fast. Winter was coming. We had to survive.

Building a Shelter Against the Storm

December 8, 1805. We started cutting trees. Sick or not, limping or not, we worked. Rain soaked us to the bone. Hands bled. Bodies broke. By December 16, we had a small fort. Walls. A roof. A fireplace. Fort Clatsop.

It wasn't home. But it was all we had.

A Cold Christmas

Christmas morning came with gunfire, not in battle, but in celebration. A few cheers. A few gifts. I made moccasins for Captain Clark. Sacagawea gave him a bundle of weasel tails. Our dinner? Spoiled elk meat. It rained all day.

We missed home, our mothers, our sweethearts, warm fires, and dry socks. But no one said it aloud.

Cold rain, cramped quarters, and months of waiting—Fort Clatsop stands as a monument to endurance on America's far frontier.

New Year's Without Joy

January 1, 1806. We woke with another volley and a half-hearted shout of "Happy New Year." Captain Clark joked that we'd grow antlers from all the elk we'd eaten. No feast. Just boiled meat and soggy biscuits.

Our bellies ached. Our clothes hung in rags. My boots were worn through, and the moss I stuffed inside was already soaked. We were freezing and tired, but we stood our watches. We did not give up.

Sickness and Sacrifice

In mid-January, Private Whitehouse had a bad tooth. The kind that makes a man scream. We pulled it while two men held him down. He passed out from the pain. Captain Lewis had studied medicine.

Sickness was everywhere. Dampness crawled into our bones. Clothes rotted right off us. Smoke from the fire never dried us, but at least it kept us alive. Most nights, I prayed, not for glory, but for one more sunrise.

Leaving the Fort

By March 1806, we were skin and bone, but still standing. The Clatsop people had taught us to carve sturdy canoes that would carry us home. On March 23, we left the fort behind.

It had rained on 106 of the 112 days we stayed. And yet, not a single man had died.

Sacagawea, with baby Jean Baptiste on her back. York, Captain Clark's enslaved servant. We had no glory. No riches. But we had our lives.

Why Fort Clatsop Still Matters

It wasn't a palace. It was wet, cold, and full of suffering. But Fort Clatsop was the turning point, where our journey west ended, and the long path home began.

We were not heroes. We were tired men with cracked hands and frostbitten feet. But we endured. That winter carved something permanent into us: courage, brotherhood, and quiet strength.

SMART TIP: Step into Private Joe's boots for a day at Fort Clatsop, **Oregon**, the winter encampment of Lewis and Clark (1805–1806). Just as we did, peek into the log cabins and touch the rough timbers, and breathe in the scent of the campfire smoke. For a moment, you might just hear the whispers of the Corps of Discovery cheering each other on through 112 rainy days.

Carson and Virginia City: Pony Express to Gold Rush

A Ride Through History

John, age 16, stumbled along the rocky trail just outside Carson City. His pony, Dusty, limped with a loose shoe, and ahead loomed the formidable Sierra Nevada Mountains. Days out from St. Joseph, **Missouri**, John carried urgent mail bound for Sacramento, **California**. Carson City, still a fledgling frontier town bustling with saloons, fortunately had a blacksmith. As John waited for Dusty's shoe to be repaired, he kept a wary eye out for bandits and Paiute warriors. Once the shoe was fixed, he grabbed his mochila, the signature mail pouch, and pressed onward. The mail had to go through. The news he carried?

The United States has a new president-elect. His name is Abraham Lincoln.

Though it operated for only 18 months, from April 1860 to October 1861, the Pony Express captured the imagination of Americans and historians alike. Today, Carson City is recognized as the premier station by the National Pony Express Association. Every June, a 10-day, nonstop horseback relay re-creates the entire 2,000-mile route. Riders, dressed in period clothing, pass the mochila from hand to hand across eight states. Their motto: "Keep the Spirit of the Pony Express Alive."

Carson City, Capital of Nevada

Named after Kit Carson, frontiersman, trapper, soldier, and Indian agent, who played a pivotal role in westward expansion.

Today, you can take a self-guided walking tour along the Kit Carson Trail, which winds through Carson City's historic district, showcasing beautifully preserved 19th-century homes and landmarks.

Don't miss the Nevada State Museum and the Carson City Mint, both rich with stories of the past. "**Nevada**" comes from the Spanish word meaning "snow-clad," a nod to the snow-capped Sierra Nevada.

Virginia City: A Living Legend

A narrow, serpentine road winds upward, twisting through hairpin curves with dramatic drop-offs and sweeping views. The route follows original wagon trails and eventually brings you to Virginia City, where the air grows thin, and history grows thick.

This town, famous for the Comstock Lode of silver and gold, feels like stepping back in time. We passed weathered wooden fences, crumbling mining shacks, and rusted equipment, a reminder of the wild rush for wealth that once defined the region.

Virginia City, with its wooden boardwalks, rustic saloons, and quaint churches, is less a city than a stage set for the Old West. We enjoyed breakfast at the Delta Saloon Café, where our meal of grits, eggs, bacon, and toast was served quickly and heartily, no fuss.

What thrilled us most, though, was learning that this very town was the launching pad for a young newspaper editor named Samuel Clemens, better known by his pen name: Mark Twain.

In 1862, with his riverboat piloting career interrupted by the Civil War, Clemens arrived in Virginia City hoping to strike it rich in the mines. But he soon realized that his true fortune lay in storytelling. Hired by the *Territorial Enterprise*, he began writing humorous and biting columns that captured the town's eccentric characters and chaotic spirit. One day, he signed an article by *Mark Twain*, a riverboat term meaning two fathoms deep. The name stuck.

Two Cities, One Frontier Spirit

Carson City and Virginia City together offer a vivid, almost theatrical experience of the Old West, where stories of grit, gold, and greatness come alive in every dusty street and mountain breeze.

SMART TIP: Start your trip in Carson City, **Nevada**, at the Kit Carson Trail, a self-guided walking tour through the historic district. Then take the winding road up to Virginia City. Drive slowly! The curves are sharp, and the roads are steep. In Virginia City, tour the Way It Was Museum, visit the Chollar Mine, and take a scenic ride on the Virginia and Truckee Railroad.

Donner Pass: Snow and Silence

(Evelyn, Natalie, and Sharlene, the oldest
daughter, traveled to the Donner Pass.)

We were told to wear boots, snow jackets, and scarves to Lake Tahoe in April. We laughed as Floridians, we don't own snow jackets. But as the howling winds swept through the gray slopes of Donner Pass, we realized that even the thickest snow gear couldn't stop the shivering.

Before us stood a towering twenty-two-foot statue on a pedestal. A family, solemn, serious, frozen in time. The father points west. The mother cradles one child in her arms while another clings to her skirts. The snow beneath our feet is a quiet witness to the terrible winter of 1846, when the snow reached the height of this statue. It's hard to believe: right here, the Donner Party was trapped. What began as a dream ended as a nightmare.

What Do You Remember About Donner Pass?

Evelyn asked a group of six teacher friends, "What do you remember about Donner Pass?"

After a pause, they all answered in unison: "Cannibalism. They ate each other. Even their children." Is that what most people remember?

The Donner Story

We turn back to the statue. George and Tamzene Donner were prosperous farmers from Springfield, **Illinois**. In 1846, they left Independence, **Missouri,** to follow the Oregon Trail. They were part of a group of nearly 90 people, later known as the Donner Party or, at times, the Donner-Reed Party, after another wealthy family who joined them, lured by promises of opportunity in **California**.

The spirit of Manifest Destiny was sweeping the country in the 1840s. Wanting to reach California quickly, they chose to break off from the main trail and follow a shortcut promoted by explorer Lansford Hastings. It was a tragic decision. The "shortcut" led them over the Sierra Nevada mountains. By early November, snow had blocked the high pass near Truckee Lake.

Donner Pass is less about what went wrong and more about what survival demands and choosing knowledge over haste.

They were stuck. Food ran out. At first, they boiled oxhide and gnawed on horse bones. But eventually, only the dead remained as a source of sustenance.

Several rescue attempts failed. The group endured not only hunger and cold but also bitter interpersonal conflicts. The final rescue party didn't arrive until March. By then, their ordeal had become a national scandal. Newspapers as far away as New York City reported the horrors in lurid detail.

Who Survived?

Historians have long studied the physical and social patterns of survival. Women survived at a much higher rate than men. Across all age groups, two-thirds of the men died, while two-thirds of the women survived. Researchers believe that women's higher body fat, typically 27% compared to 15% in men, helped insulate them from the cold. Lower metabolic rates and less aggression may also have helped.

Interestingly, of the 30 men who died, about 13% were victims of violence, fights that broke out under the strain of survival. Some scholars believe interpersonal conflict was an even greater threat than the weather.

Family connections mattered. Every single man over 21 who traveled alone died. No adults over 45 survived. Among children under five, 62.5% perished, but among those aged 6 to 14, only 2 out of 21 died.

Many books have been written about the Donner Party. But nothing brings it home like the stark displays at the Visitor Center outside of Lake Tahoe.

A Cold Reminder

Standing before the cold, rough stone of the monument, we feel its chill, not just in our bones but in our hearts. It is as unforgiving as the winter that sealed their fate.

"They were just ordinary people," Sharlene said. "They weren't heroes. They weren't villains. They were desperate. They did what they had to."

Natalie nods. "And they were forever judged for it."

We stand silently, humbled and sad. Then Evelyn adds, "We have it so easy. Great highways. Heated cars. Grocery stores."

As we turn to leave, we glance back at the statue one last time. And just beyond it, from a nearby building, a gas station sign glows brightly, modern comfort looming over a tragic past.

SMART TIPS: Tip #1: This impatience to get to **California** led to interpersonal conflict and irrational decisions. Before traveling, do your research, make informed decisions, and ask professionals.

Tip #2: Don't judge history through the lens of today. Instead, ask yourself: *What would I have done in the cold winter of 1846?*

Abraham Lincoln and Jefferson Davis: Two Boys from Kentucky

Kentucky, the Bluegrass State, is famous for its fast horses, Churchill Downs, the vast underground wonder of Mammoth Cave, and a certain world-famous fried chicken (yes, KFC).

But **Kentucky** holds another, less talked-about distinction: it was the birthplace of two boys who would one day lead opposing sides in one of the most painful chapters in American history. The conflict has been called many names: the Civil War, the War Between the States, and even the War of Northern Aggression.

Kentucky in the Early 1800s

What was life like in **Kentucky** in the early 19th century? In a word, rough. This frontier land was wild and untamed. Families who crossed the Appalachian Mountains to settle here were true pioneers, carving out a hard life in a rugged land.

It was into this world that two boys were born, just a year and about 100 miles apart. Each would rise to national leadership. One would become president of the United States and lead the Union. The other would become president of the Confederate States.

Different Beginnings

Abraham Lincoln was born on February 12, 1809, in a one-room log cabin near Hodgenville, **Kentucky**. His parents were poor farmers, and he spent his youth doing manual labor. Though he attended school for less than a year, he developed a deep love of learning and lived by the pioneer values of perseverance, honesty, and hard work.

As a young man, Lincoln moved to **Illinois**, working a variety of jobs before teaching himself law. He entered politics, losing more elections than he won, until he rose to national prominence. In 1860, the newly formed Republican Party chose him as its candidate for president.

Jefferson Davis, born June 3, 1808, in Fairview, **Kentucky**, came from a more privileged background. His family owned a large plantation and eventually relocated to **Mississippi**. Davis received a classical education and graduated from the U.S. Military Academy at West Point in 1828. He married the daughter of General Zachary Taylor and served with distinction in the Mexican War. Like Lincoln, he entered politics, serving in both the U.S. House and Senate.

Brothers on Opposing Sides

In 1861, Abraham Lincoln became the 16th president of the United States. His mission: to preserve the Union. Jefferson Davis—believing in states' rights and in a Southern way of life that tragically depended on slavery—was chosen as president of the newly formed Confederate States of America.

Kentucky, though a slave state, did not secede. As a border state, it was deeply divided, families split, loyalties torn. Both Union flags and Confederate "Stars and Bars" flew over **Kentucky** soil.

The war was brutal. Over 600,000 Americans died. Towns burned, families were fractured, and a nation bled.

In April 1865, General Robert E. Lee surrendered, marking the war's end. Just days later, one of **Kentucky**'s native sons, Abraham Lincoln, was assassinated at Ford's Theatre in Washington, D.C.

After the War

The aftermath was complicated. Lincoln had envisioned a generous plan for Southern reconstruction, but his death changed the course. Jefferson Davis was captured in **Georgia**, imprisoned for two years, and charged with treason, but never tried. He spent his final years at Beauvoir in Biloxi, **Mississippi**, and died in 1889. Beauvoir is now a memorial library.

Lincoln, meanwhile, is honored with a towering memorial at the western end of the National Mall in Washington, D.C.

Two boys, born a year apart in the same rugged state, grew into leaders who shaped a nation, for better and for worse.

SMART TIP: Kentucky remembers both of its famous sons. In Fairview, you can visit the Jefferson Davis State Historic Site, marked by a towering obelisk. In Hodgenville, the Abraham Lincoln Birthplace National Historical Park preserves the humble beginnings of a future president.

Shiloh, Vicksburg, Gettysburg: Ghosts of the Civil War Battlefields

When you walk across a Civil War battlefield, the silence itself feels alive. It's not just the monuments or the rolling fields that capture you, but the strange weight of the past. These are landscapes where thousands of men fell, and many say their spirits remain. Whether or not you believe in ghosts, the stories of these battlefields linger like morning fog and are impossible to ignore.

Shiloh, Tennessee: The Peach Orchard and the Sunken Road

The name *Shiloh* means "place of peace," yet in April of 1862, it was anything but. In two days of savage fighting, over 23,700 men were killed, wounded, or missing. The battle raged through peach orchards, along the Tennessee River, and across a sunken farm road where soldiers fell in heaps.

When we visited, the serenity of the countryside felt almost deceptive. Standing at the edge of the Sunken Road, we thought of the soldiers who never left it, and for a moment the silence pressed down heavy, as if asking us not to forget. Some visitors have reported hearing phantom drumbeats or cries for help. While others reported seeing a lone soldier in a Confederate uniform walking near the Peach Orchard at dusk, vanishing when approached.

The landscape is beautiful, but it whispers of something unfinished.

Vicksburg, Mississippi: A City Under Siege

If Shiloh was sudden and bloody, Vicksburg was slow and merciless. In 1863, Union forces surrounded the "Gibraltar of the Confederacy," bombarding the city for 47 days. Civilians dug caves into the hills to survive, living underground as shells blasted overhead.

Walking the rolling hills of the Vicksburg National Military Park, we were struck by the cannons perched in silent lines, their barrels aimed as if still waiting for the next volley. The *USS Cairo*, raised from the riverbed, stood like a ghost ship with its iron frame both robust and skeletal. At one point, a heavy mist drifted over the bluffs, and the battlefield felt cloaked in memory. Locals say soldiers still march here at night, their footsteps echoing in the fog. As we stood by the river at sunset, the water glowing with orange light, we could almost imagine them, shadows keeping watch over the city they once fought to defend.

Gettysburg, Pennsylvania:
The Turning Point and the Most Haunted

Gettysburg is the crown jewel of Civil War battlefields. Over three days in July 1863, over 51,000 men were killed, wounded, or missing. The battle shifted the tide of the war, but it also left behind a spiritual scar.

When we walked through The Wheatfield, the air was still. It's hard to picture now, with tall grass swaying in the breeze, but this was once a place where the ground ran red. Devil's Den felt heavy too; the great boulders seemed to lean in close, as though keeping secrets. Some visitors report ghostly figures, strange mists and shapes in photographs, or the sound of gunfire when none is there. We didn't hear musket fire, but we did feel the weight of eyes upon us, as if history itself was watching.

In town, the ghost stories are woven into the very fabric of daily life. We joined a candlelit walking tour one evening, wandering past brick houses that once served as hospitals. The guide's lantern light flickered against old walls, and the air seemed to carry both the laughter of modern visitors and the faint echo of groans from long ago. Whether or not one believes in spirits, Gettysburg's presence is undeniable.

Where History Refuses to Die

Civil War battlefields are more than historic sites; they are sacred ground. They remind us that America's story was written in sacrifice, blood, and grief. For some, these fields are haunted by restless soldiers. For others, the "ghosts" are simply memories too strong to fade.

As travelers, we came to see history, but we left with something more. In these fields, you don't just learn about the past; you feel it. The silence speaks, and if you pause long enough, you may hear it too.

SMART TIP: Before visiting any Civil War battlefield, stop at the Visitor Center. These mini-museums offer short films, detailed maps, and guided tours by Park Rangers that help bring history and humanity to life. Some battlefields offer driving tours with audio guides you can follow at your own pace.

Boot Hill:
Final Stop of the Frontier

By Sharlene Chatham, as told to Evelyn

S harlene is thrilled to be in **Montana**, with its towering mountains, vast plains, and rugged badlands. She is delighted to be under the biggest sky she has ever seen. And under that sky is an exceptional treat- Boot Hill.

What is Boot Hill?

Boot Hill is the epitome of lawlessness in the Old West of the 1800s. Western movies have romanticized the trials and tribulations of gunslingers, bank robbers, and lawmen who met their fate. Boot Hill is not one specific place but a general term for frontier-era cemeteries across the West. These places are called Boot Hill for the people who died and were buried with their boots on. Many died violently or suddenly, often from gunfights. Dozens of boot hills have been forgotten; a few have become famous.

Other well-known sites are also well preserved, and each has fascinating stories. Established in 1878, Tombstone, **Arizona**, is a major tourist attraction with 250-300 burials. It is famous for the O.K. Corral. And other famous sites are in Dodge City, **Kansas**, and Virginia City, **Montana.**

Then-Coulson; Now-Billings, Montana

As Sharlene climbed the hill and reached the top, she was quiet, surrounded by the history that encircled them. No one else was there. It was the remnant of an authentic ghost town.

She gazed across the hillside dotted with crumbling small sandstone markers. She could picture the town of Coulson and imagined their stories. So many lives ended here.

Two Notables

How unusual, there is a huge marker on the Hill with a name on it. It is the grave of H. M. "Muggins" Taylor. His claim to fame is that he delivered news of Custer's last stand at the Battle of the Little Bighorn. Later, he became a sheriff in the town and was called to a disturbance at a local laundry. A drunk was threatening to kill his wife, and Muggins was called to intervene. Sadly, he was shot and died. He was buried on Boot Hill but given a proper funeral without his boots on.

Another notable is Luther "Yellowstone" Kelly. He was a rugged frontiersman and scout who explored the Yellowstone Country from 1869 to 1885. He requested that he be buried in Boot Hill.

Little Girl in an Unmarked Grave

So many poignant stories could be told about the many small mounds of earth with no stone or fence. However, a 1936 WPA survey project revealed the story of a child, about 10 years old, found frozen in the winter of 1881-82; the child's name is unknown, likely an orphan from a wagon party. The body was laid to rest on the hill with others; a kind woman gave her a calico dress for burial.

As Sharlene descended the lonely hill, she realized Boot Hill is not just a relic on a mountain but a testament to the marvelous history of our nation and the people who shaped it.

Leaving the Hill, she spied a large crowd. The Oscar Meyer Wienermobile had parked, and people were taking selfies of the large Wiener truck, amazed at seeing such a marvelous sight.

She couldn't get near the Oscar Meyer Wienermobile, but was alone on Boot Hill. Is history fair?

SMART TIP: When visiting the West, make time to explore Boot Hill cemeteries; they are quiet, evocative reminders of frontier life.

Nashville: The Vote that Changed America

Nashville, **Tennessee**, is home to Country music and the Grand Ole Opry, as well as historical places such as the Hermitage and Belle Meade, and the magnificent Parthenon, a replica of the famous site in Athens, Greece. **Tennessee** is an old state admitted to the Union on June 1, 1796.

It is also Evelyn's home state.

But although Music City and **Tennessee** history are exciting, it is also home to an important event and one man's vote that changed America.

Meet Harry Burn (story from Harry's point of view, adapted by Evelyn)

*Hi, I am Harry, and I'm only 24. It's a thrill to be elected the youngest person to the **Tennessee** House of Representatives from McMinn County.*

Usually, our sessions are quiet, but not this year. It is 1920, and the streets of Nashville are mobbed. Governor A. H. Roberts has called a special session of the state congress to vote on the 19th Amendment, women's right to vote. These advocates were called suffragettes. Both sides lobbied, petitioned, blackmailed, and even prayed over the legislature.

Background

The U.S. Congress had passed the 19th Amendment on June 4, 1919, and sent it to the states for ratification. Over the last 14 months, **Illinois, Wisconsin, and Michigan** ratified, followed by other states, bringing the total to 35 states. Thirty-six states were needed for ratification.

*Now, the area I came from in East **Tennessee** was divided, and I wanted to please my supporters, many of whom were against it. So, I donned the red rose, showing that I was against the women's right to vote. A yellow rose meant "yes."*

Sitting in my hotel, I had read a letter from my mother, Febb Ensminger Burn. She told me to "be a good boy" and vote for the ratification. I snickered at the good boy bit and put the letter in my pocket.

In the legislative chamber, it was chaotic. It was hot. I listened, but began to think, my mother knows more about politics than most men; why should she not be able to vote? Women have been managing households and working through the years to make our country great. I will do the right thing.

It was a roll-call vote, and one by one, it would be tight 38-38, and a tie meant a no vote.

Then my name was called. I fumbled with the letter in my pocket.

I said, "AYE."

SILENCE. With my one word, Tennessee became the 36th state to ratify the 19th Amendment, women's right to vote.

The backlash was swift. I was accused of being a traitor by one side and praised by the other. But the letter from my mother was dear. I was able to sleep at night thinking I had been "a good boy." Would I do it again- AYE.

A quiet moment that changed a nation, Harry Burn and his mother, Febb, whose words and courage turned one son's vote into a turning point for American women.

Thoughts in 2026

Tennessee is proud of its significant role in the women's suffrage movement. In Centennial Park, a monument was unveiled to commemorate **Tennessee**'s crucial role in ratifying the Amendment; a historical marker is also located outside the Hermitage Hotel.

Evelyn often thinks of the humble young man and his courageous mother, who helped make this the 36th state to grant women the right to vote and run for office. Her mother, from East **Tennessee**, never voted, but her father encouraged this young girl to be interested in politics. She even made her first political speech in the 5th grade. She could not register until the age of 21, but went down on her 21st birthday to fill out the credentials. (Now, most states have the age of 18).

And Evelyn attributes this book to Harry and Febb Burn, who enabled her to run for office in 1992. She lost by a few votes, but her husband said, "Go travel —you deserve it." That led this mother and daughter to write two books: *Have a Love Affair with Travel and Have a Love Affair with the USA.*

Harry and Febb Burn, you are appreciated.

SMART TIP: In Nashville, walk the path of history. Visit Centennial Park's Women's Suffrage Monument and the Hermitage Hotel, where the "War of the Roses" decided women's right to vote. Visit the **Tennessee** State Museum (free) for the actual red/yellow roses and Febb's letter replica. Remember Harry Burn—one young man, guided by his mother's letter, proved that one voice can change the world.

Oak Ridge: The Secret City of Science

The southern Appalachian Mountains guard many secrets within their rugged ridges and thick forests. This was once the land of the Cherokee, whose treaties were broken, and later home to hardy settlers who braved the elements to carve out a living. Their lives were changed forever when the Tennessee Valley Authority built dams that flooded farmlands and homesteads. Yet, the resilient people of East **Tennessee** endured, unaware of an even greater secret taking shape beneath their feet.

The Atom's Shadow – 1945

"Wake up, baby," Evelyn's daddy said. "The bomb that was just dropped on Japan was created at Oak Ridge."

Evelyn was just a child then, growing up in Knoxville, only 30 miles from a secret city that no one knew existed. Its name wasn't on any map. Its purpose was unknown. But that morning, the world changed, and suddenly, Oak Ridge was the talk of our lives, so close and yet so mysterious.

The world was still at war. Germany had surrendered, but Japan remained defiant. An invasion seemed inevitable, with horrifying projections of casualties on both sides. Far from the front lines, however, another battle raged, the race to harness the atom before our enemies could.

The Secret Arises

In 1938, two German scientists discovered how to split the uranium atom. American physicists realized the devastating potential if Hitler were to gain that power. The U.S. responded with urgency. In 1942, the top-secret Manhattan Project was born.

In the high desert of Los Alamos, **New Mexico**, brilliant minds like theoretical physicist J. Robert Oppenheimer worked in silence. General Leslie Groves, a man known for cutting through red tape, oversaw another crucial task, uranium enrichment in the hills of East **Tennessee**. That work advanced to Hanford, **Washington**, where giant reactors produced plutonium. The clock was ticking.

On July 16, 1945, the desert of **New Mexico** erupted with light and fire. The first atomic bomb had been detonated. The Manhattan Project had succeeded.

Oak Ridge: A City Born in Secrecy

Oak Ridge was placed on maps in late 1945.

But before that, tens of thousands had moved there almost overnight, living behind barbed wire fences, guarded entrances, and a vow of silence. Many workers didn't even know what the person next to them was doing, and they didn't ask. They didn't know they were helping to split atoms to build the most powerful weapon the world had ever seen.

That all changed in August 1945. When "Little Boy" was dropped on Hiroshima and "Fat Man" on Nagasaki, the workers of Oak Ridge suddenly understood the true purpose of their labor.

Despite the secrecy, life went on. Families attended church, children went to school, and played past buildings marked "Caution: Radiation." Victory gardens grew in backyards, and dances lit up the evenings. After the war, outsiders could finally visit the town, often jokingly referred to as "high-class slums" due to its hastily built, prefabricated housing.

Today's Oak Ridge: Where Hope Meets Science

Years later, Evelyn visited Oak Ridge with a group of science writers. What a transformation.

Oak Ridge remains at the forefront of scientific discovery. The Oak Ridge National Laboratory conducts groundbreaking research in energy, health, materials science, and national security. This once-secret city is now filled with parks, greenways, thriving neighborhoods, and a palpable sense of community pride.

Plan Your Visit to Oak Ridge

Begin at the American Museum of Science and Energy (AMSE), where interactive exhibits and original Manhattan Project equipment bring history to life. Stand before a massive Calutron, once operated by the "Calutron Girls" who unknowingly helped shape history. Then, take a bus tour to the Y-12 National Security Complex and the graphite reactor—the birthplace of atomic energy. End your visit at Historic Jackson Square and the International Friendship Bell, a moving symbol of peace and reconciliation.

SMART TIP: Visit AMSE and the X-10 Graphite Reactor (open Thu–Sat). Download the Oak Ridge Secret City app for self-guided driving tours of historic gates, cemeteries, and "alphabet houses." For Y-12 history, watch the DOE virtual tour online. Pair with Frozen Head State Park (30 min away), rugged trails once patrolled by Manhattan Project guards.

Pair your trip to Oak Ridge with a visit to the Great Smoky Mountains National Park. In one journey, you will witness the grandeur of untouched nature, and in the other, the achievements of human ingenuity.

From Apollo to Artemis: Space Travel Then and Now

July 20, 1969

Some 600 million viewers gathered in front of their black-and-white television sets. Something extraordinary was happening 240,000 miles away. A crackling voice came through:

"Houston, Tranquility Base here. The Eagle has landed."

They were witnessing history, the Apollo 11 Moon landing. And then came a moment the world would never forget. Neil Armstrong stepped onto the powdery lunar surface and declared:

"That's one small step for man, one giant leap for mankind."

This Moon landing was more than a scientific feat—it was a triumph of spirit, imagination, and courage. Seeing the American flag planted on the lunar surface filled us with pride and a sense of purpose. It made the impossible feel possible and sparked generations of curiosity.

Now, decades later, we're about to explore how that magic happened and where it's headed next.

Visit to the U.S. Space & Rocket Center: Huntsville, Alabama

Standing beneath a 363-foot-long Saturn V rocket, longer than a football field, is humbling. A knowledgeable docent walks us through its three powerful stages:

- **Stage I** – Liftoff and initial ascent (about 2.5 minutes), built at NASA's Michoud Assembly Facility in New Orleans, **Louisiana**.
- **Stage II** – Continued ascent through the upper atmosphere (about 6 minutes), built by North American Aviation in Seal Beach, **California**.
- **Stage III** – Orbit insertion and lunar trajectory, built by Douglas Aircraft in Huntington Beach, **California**.

Each stage was tested at NASA Marshall Space Flight Center in Huntsville, then sent to the Kennedy Space Center in **Florida** for assembly and launch.

What You'll See

Like any great museum, this one is packed with wonders: photographs, slideshows, interactive displays, and even hands-on astronaut experiences.

- **Apollo 16 Command Module**
  The actual spacecraft that orbited the Moon in 1972. It's small, scorched, and legendary. Peering inside, we marveled at how tight the space was and imagined what it must have felt like to be inside.
- **Astronaut Training Simulators**
  We watched Space Camp students test their courage on a G-force accelerator, multi-axis trainer, and moonwalk simulator. These contraptions test your nerves and your stomach!
- **International Space Station Replica**
  A full-scale lab module shows how astronauts live and work in space. You'll find sleeping quarters, exercise stations, and even a zero-gravity toilet.

Let's just say we're glad we chose a profession with gravity.

Rocket Park

Even in the summer heat, it's worth strolling through the outdoor Rocket Park, featuring more than two dozen historic rockets and missiles. Smooth walking paths and benches make this a relaxing, inspiring walk through the history of space.

What's Next in Space?

Once, traveling to the Moon seemed like science fiction. Now, the future of space exploration is unfolding right before our eyes:

- **Artemis Program** – Returning astronauts to the Moon in phases.
- **NASA's Perseverance Rover** – Already exploring Mars, collecting soil samples.
- **SpaceX Starship** – Aiming to send humans to Mars.
- **Space Tourism & Lunar Mining** – Private space stations, asteroid mining, and luxury orbital travel are in development.
- **James Webb Space Telescope** – Offering an awe-inspiring look into galaxies, exoplanets, and perhaps signs of life.
- **Smart Robots & Rovers** – Becoming more intelligent and capable of performing complex tasks beyond Earth.

Space is no longer just the realm of science fiction; it's becoming part of the human story. Who knows where the next frontier will take us?

SMART TIP: Book timed tickets for Huntsville's Rocket Center. Check the NASA app for Kennedy Space Center launches. Or, become an Armchair Adventurer: track live missions, explore space through online tours, and follow NASA's updates from the comfort of your living room.

Presidential Libraries: America's Living Legacy

This article originated from a suggestion made by a participant during our speaking engagement at Academia Hernando, **Florida**. A well-groomed lady shared that she and her husband had traveled the world, explored all 50 states, and yet something still felt missing. Their answer? They decided to visit every presidential library.

What a marvelous idea! Organized by region, these presidential libraries are more than collections of books—they are living museums of Americana. Each one offers a window into the life, times, and legacy of a U.S. president. Some are part of the National Archives and Records Administration (NARA), while others are state-run institutions that hold just as much fascination.

Each library is organized by region. Some of the libraries have a more inclusive commentary by Richard Ramos, a political operative and researcher from **New York**, whose comments are in italics.

EAST COAST

John F. Kennedy Presidential Library and Museum, Boston, **Massachusetts:** Jacqueline *Kennedy Onassis played an intimate role in the design of the library and its architecture. This was the first presidential library to offer a gift shop with a variety of Kennedy memorabilia. This includes a replica of his rocking chair, clothing, PT 109 tie pins, etc.*

Calvin Coolidge Presidential Library and Museum, Northampton, **Massachusetts**: Located in Forbes Library, this gem reflects "Silent Cal" in a charming New England town.

Franklin Delano Roosevelt Presidential Library and Museum, Hyde Park, **New York**: *Eleanor Roosevelt oversaw the development of the FDR library and museum. Located at Hyde Park, the library and museum are together beside his home, on the Hudson River. They focus on President Roosevelt's use of communication as a way to comfort Americans suffering during the Great Depression with his "Fireside Chats."*

There are numerous photos, audio, and video recordings about the great buildup to World War II, a discussion of the Axis powers, and the global threat of Adolf Hitler. There is a section dedicated to the attack on Pearl Harbor.

Barack Obama Presidential Center, Chicago, **Illinois**, Jackson Park: The first 21st-century digital library, blending museum and community space.

MIDWEST

Herbert Hoover Library, West Branch, **Iowa**: From Iowa boy to humanitarian president during the Great Depression. Don't miss his two-room birthplace cottage.

Dwight D. Eisenhower Library, Abilene, **Kansas**: Visit Ike's childhood home and WWII military displays.

Harry S. Truman Presidential Library and Museum, Independence, **Missouri**: Learn how a small-town man ended WWII and guided America into the Cold War.

Gerald R. Ford Presidential Library and Museum, Ann Arbor & Grand Rapids, **Michigan**: President Ford's unique split-site library covers the turbulent 1970s.

President Harry S. Truman's Key West home, less a presidential library and more a lived-in retreat, where his memoirs come to life, and visitors can ride through town in his former limousine.

Rutherford B. Hayes Presidential Library and Museum (not NARA), Fremont, **Ohio**: The first presidential library (1890 cornerstone; dedicated 1916), with a Victorian mansion and genealogy center.

Abraham Lincoln Presidential Library and Museum (not NARA), Springfield, **Illinois**: State-run, with multimedia exhibits on Lincoln's life and the Civil War.

SOUTH

Jimmy Carter Presidential Library and Museum, Atlanta, **Georgia**: From peanut farmer to Nobel Peace Prize winner. A beautiful facility that focuses on peace and shows the Camp David Accords and Carter's humanitarian legacy.

Ulysses S. Grant Presidential Library (not NARA), Starkville, **Mississippi**: The home of Grant's library, which showcases Civil War and Reconstruction exhibits, including official presidential papers.

William J. Clinton Presidential Library and Museum, Little Rock, **Arkansas**: A striking modern building on the Arkansas River, showcasing the booming 1990s.

Lyndon B. Johnson Presidential Library, Austin, **Texas**: *President Johnson played an active role in creating the library and used it to correct what he felt were misconceptions about himself and his presidency. A great deal of the library space focuses on the President's "Great Society" initiative, which he saw as the logical successor to President Franklin Roosevelt's New Deal and President Truman's Fair Deal. A most stunning perspective is a series of fountain pens that circle from the ground floor to the top floor, and each pen reflects a piece of legislation signed by the President, showing that the passage of major legislation in Congress is unmatched.*

There is a section dedicated to the assassination of President Kennedy with audio recordings from Lady Bird Johnson, Governor Connally, and Nellie Connally, who were riding in President Kennedy's limousine when the fateful shots were fired.

The collection also includes recordings of phone calls made from Air Force One to the Kennedy Family and others as the plane returned to Washington, D.C. In the library, there are black telephone receivers, and if you pick them up, you can listen to conversations with different historical figures. The calls are placed in subheading sections of the library, such as civil rights, where you can listen to discussions with Reverend Dr. Martin Luther King, Jr., and others.

A very stark element of the library is a section of the library which deals with Vietnam, and an exhibit that was made with service member dog tags representing all who were killed in action and wounded.

George H.W. Bush Presidential Library and Museum (Bush 41), College Station, **Texas**: President George H.W. Bush Library, located in College Station, Texas, 90 miles northwest of Houston, reflects the 41st President, his history and legacy, as well as his accomplishments. However, unlike other Presidential libraries, which are shrines to the men, this library reflects on the "Greatest Generation," the term coined by journalist Tom Brokaw.

A replica of the plane he flew during World War II is on display, along with the video of his rescue from the Pacific.

George W. Bush Presidential Library and Museum (Bush 43), Dallas, **Texas**: Includes a moving 9/11 memorial and an interactive "Decision Points Theater."

WEST

Richard Nixon Presidential Library and Museum—Yorba Linda, **California**: *The Nixon Library emphasizes foreign policy and Nixon's upbringing in this former farming community, not far from Anaheim and Disneyland. The highlight includes the Marine One helicopter, which took President and Mrs. Nixon to Andrews Air Force Base on the day of the resignation.*

Ronald Reagan Presidential Library—Simi Valley, **California**:

*The Reagan Library is stunning in its architecture, and its scenic location in the Santa Susana Mountains in Simi Valley is breathtaking. It serves as a monument to the "Great Communicator," showcasing his life through pictures, videos, and audio recordings. An impressive effort is made to recreate Reagan's early years in Dixon, **Illinois**. Then it traces his story through Hollywood, his time as Union President, his campaign for **California** Governor, his loss to Gerald Ford for the 1976 Presidential*

Natalie and Evelyn sit at President Ronald Reagan's desk with Paul Leoni, supporter of the Ronald Reagan Presidential Library.

nomination, and his eventual victory as President. It covers his White House years, travels while in office, and provides perspectives on his life from Camp David, his ranch in the hills, and his final years.

Evelyn and Natalie share their favorite memories of the Reagan library, including speaking at his presidential podium, sitting at his desk in a replica of the Oval Office, touring Air Force One, and paying respect to him at his final resting place.

More Than Paper

Presidential libraries are more than repositories of papers and artifacts—they are places where history speaks, where triumphs and trials are preserved, and where visitors step into the very moments that shaped America. Whether in a quiet New England town, a Midwestern prairie, or beneath **California**'s vast skies, each library is a chapter in the unfolding story of our nation.

SMART TIP: Plan ahead when visiting a presidential library. Check the library's website to buy tickets in advance, especially for popular sites like the Reagan Library. Combo ticket: Buy the Presidential Libraries Passport and stamp at each site. Also, download the NARA Presidential Libraries app for audio tours, declassified docs, and virtual JFK phone calls.

PART 3

Culture and People Define a Nation

More than landscapes and landmarks, it is the people who define a nation. In this chapter, we explore stories of love and friendship that celebrate the human heart. Here are moments of connection, courage, and compassion, individuals whose creativity, kindness, or quiet strength left the world a little better than they found it. These are the faces and stories that remind us why every journey is, at its core, about people.

Love Affairs <u>IN</u> the USA

Our book is titled *Have a Love Affair with the USA*. We write about American history, its wars, landscapes, and stories from sea to shining sea. Yet, woven into the nation's fabric are tales not only of courage and ambition but also of love. Romance, devotion, and partnership are as central to America's story as its battles, inventions, and explorations.

Some of these love stories are legendary, others preserved in letters, literature, or memory. They capture not only the romance between two people but also the spirit of a time and place. From presidents and first ladies to musicians, writers, and everyday dreamers, American love stories reveal resilience, longing, loyalty, and sometimes heartbreak.

Here are six unforgettable American love stories:

1. Abigail and John Adams –
America's First Power Couple (Massachusetts)
Their story began unremarkably. John dismissed her at first, and Abigail hardly noticed the short, plump man with thinning hair. But over three years, admiration grew into affection, and they married in 1764, riding together on a single horse to their new home. Their marriage lasted 50 years, surviving long separations during the Revolutionary War and the birth of a new nation. Through it all, they wrote over 1,160 letters, revealing themselves as lovers, partners, advisers, and confidants. Those letters endure as a testament to their bond.

2. Johnny Cash and June Carter –
Music and Redemption (Tennessee)

Few romances in music history shine brighter. June Carter, already famous from her family's folk group, met Johnny Cash at the Grand Ole Opry. Both were married at the time and facing personal struggles. June described life with Johnny as standing in a "ring of fire," words that became the title of a hit song. Arrested seven times for drugs and alcohol, Johnny nearly lost everything, but June's steadfast love helped him overcome addiction. In 1968, he proposed onstage before 7,000 fans. They married soon after and spent more than 30 years together, a love stitched with both turbulence and grace.

3. Ronald and Nancy Reagan –
Hollywood's Sweethearts (California)

Their romance began when Nancy, mistakenly blacklisted in Hollywood, sought Ron's help as president of the Screen Actors Guild. Attraction sparked, but it took three years before he proposed. They married in 1952, and Nancy became his anchor, through Hollywood, his governorship, and his two-term presidency. She famously stood by him after an assassination attempt and later became his devoted caregiver as he battled Alzheimer's. Their marriage, tender and enduring, stood as one of America's most public love stories.

4. Jimmy and Rosalynn Carter –
A Lifetime of Love (Georgia)

Their marriage was the longest presidential marriage, spanning more than seven decades. Childhood neighbors in Plains, **Georgia**, they reconnected when Jimmy, home from the Naval Academy, took Rosalynn to a movie in 1945. They wed the following year. Rosalynn worked beside him on the peanut farm, in campaigns, and in the White House. Afterward, they dedicated their lives to humanitarian work through the Carter Center. Even in his final years, their devotion never wavered. Jimmy lived to be 100, Rosalynn lived to be 96; their story is one of partnership as much as passion.

5. Martin Luther King Jr. and Coretta Scott – A Dream Shared (Georgia)

In Boston, Martin was a theology student; Coretta, a gifted musician. They bonded over music, philosophy, and a shared vision of justice. Married in 1953 in her family's **Alabama** backyard, they faced the trials of leadership, public scrutiny, and constant danger. Coretta raised their children and advanced the civil rights movement alongside her husband. Their marriage endured until Martin's assassination in 1968, after which Coretta carried his dream forward with unshakable strength.

6. Mark Twain and Olivia Langdon – A Writer's Pursuit (Many States)

Samuel Clemens, better known as Mark Twain, was rough-hewn, adventurous, and from a modest background. Olivia Langdon was refined, educated, and the daughter of a wealthy family. Twain fell in love with her portrait before meeting her. When he proposed within two weeks, she refused. He tried again and failed. Only after a staged carriage accident, in which Olivia nursed him, did she finally agree. Determined to be the husband she deserved, Twain read the Bible daily and curbed his rough ways. Their marriage was one of balance: her refinement and his humor sustaining them through joys and hardships alike.

SMART TIP: When visiting landmarks, pause to uncover the love stories behind them. Romance often shaped history: from the letters of Abigail and John Adams to the melodies of Johnny and June. Knowing the hearts behind the heroes makes every monument, museum, and melody come alive with deeper meaning.

St. Simons Island:
A Slave Boy, a Master's Son, and a Bond That Endured

The coast of **Georgia** is adorned with barrier islands known for their unspoiled beaches, world-class golf courses, deep-sea fishing charters, luxury spas, and vibrant culinary scenes. Among these, the Golden Isles—Sea Island, Jekyll Island, Little St. Simons Island, and St. Simons Island—stand out as treasures of natural beauty and rich history. St. Simons Island, in particular, enchants visitors with its historic lighthouse, reputedly haunted, that adds a touch of mystery to its coastal charm.

Yet amid this idyllic landscape lies a moving tale of love and friendship that has echoed through the generations.

1831: St. Simons Island – A Place of Isolation

Anna King inherited Retreat Plantation, one of **Georgia**'s most prominent estates, known for its production of long-staple cotton. Alongside her husband, a U.S. Congressman, she managed the plantation, which, like others of its kind, relied on enslaved labor.

In these remote surroundings, children often had few companions. It was common practice to pair young plantation heirs with enslaved children as playmates. Henry Lord Page King, affectionately called "Lordy," was paired with Neptune Small, a boy of similar age who was enslaved on the plantation. Despite the vast gulf between their stations, the two boys became inseparable. They roamed the swamps, fished, and hunted together. Anna King, unusually progressive for her time, taught both boys to read and write, strengthening a bond that defied the rigid boundaries of their world.

1861: The Shadow of War

When the Civil War broke out in 1861, coastal **Georgia** was swept into the conflict. Lordy joined the Confederate Army, and Neptune chose to accompany him, not as a soldier but as a steadfast companion.

Together, they endured the brutal march of war through the Peninsula Campaign, Richmond, Sharpsburg in **Maryland**, and Harpers Ferry in **West Virginia**. On December 13, 1862, during the Battle of Fredericksburg, Lordy volunteered for a dangerous mission and was fatally shot. In the chaos that followed, Neptune searched the battlefield until he found Lordy's body. Refusing to leave his friend behind, Neptune secured a pine coffin and arranged for Lordy's temporary burial in Savannah, **Georgia**.

Best friends, Neptune, the son of a slave, carries the body of Lordy, the son of a plantation owner, from the battlefield. This moment honors friendship, sacrifice, and shared humanity.

A Free Man's Choice

Later that year, Neptune Small was declared a free man. Yet, instead of beginning a new life elsewhere, he returned to the Confederate front to care for Tip, the youngest of the King sons.

Years later, after the war ended, Neptune again returned to Savannah. He exhumed Lordy's remains and brought him home to St. Simons Island, where Lordy was laid to rest in the family plot at Christ Church.

In gratitude for his loyalty, the King family granted Neptune a parcel of land, where he built a home. That land would eventually become Neptune Park, named in his honor. He lived a long life and passed away in 1907 at the age of 75.

Today: Remembering Neptune's Legacy

Neptune Small is buried in the cemetery for enslaved persons on the grounds of Retreat Plantation. It is now situated beside the ninth hole of the exclusive Sea Island Golf Course, one of the most prestigious in the country.

His story and the enduring bond between him and Lordy remain among the most touching chapters in the history of St. Simons Island. A bronze statue of Neptune now stands in Neptune Park, a powerful tribute to friendship, loyalty, and the human spirit's capacity to rise above the circumstances of its time.

SMART TIP: Visit Neptune Park on St. Simons Island and pause by the plaque of Neptune Small. It's more than a scenic stop; it's a quiet reminder that love and loyalty can transcend even the harshest divides of history.

Wright Brothers: Two Little Boys from Ohio to the Skies of Kitty Hawk

We are traveling down the Outer Banks of **North Carolina**, a slender thread of land flanked by shimmering waters and a striking reminder of its vulnerability to hurricanes. Yet beyond its natural beauty, the Outer Banks hold immense historical significance: from the mystery of the Lost Colony to the towering Cape Hatteras Lighthouse, the tallest in North America. However, most inspiring of all is the Wright Brothers National Memorial in Kitty Hawk.

A Childhood Spark

Wilbur Wright (1867) and Orville Wright (1871) grew up in Dayton, **Ohio,** in a home where curiosity and invention were encouraged. Their father, Milton, a minister, and their mother, Susan, a mechanically gifted woman, nurtured their natural inquisitiveness.

But a small toy changed the course of their lives. In 1878, their father brought home a rubber-band-powered helicopter, designed by French aviation pioneer Alphonse Pénaud. That tiny flying machine lit a spark in the young brothers that would burn for a lifetime.

From Bicycles to Flight

Their curiosity didn't end with childhood. Though neither brother finished high school, their mechanical talents led them to open the

Wright Cycle Company in 1892. Repairing and building bicycles not only supported them financially but sharpened the engineering skills they would later apply to aviation.

By the late 1890s, their attention had shifted skyward. They studied aviation pioneers like Otto Lilienthal and Samuel Langley, quickly grasping that successful flight required mastering three principles: lift, drag, and control. With characteristic discipline, they began experimenting, first with kites and gliders, then with wind tunnels of their own design to test new ideas.

The Winds of Kitty Hawk

Seeking the right conditions for flight, the Wright brothers selected Kitty Hawk, **North Carolina**, for its steady winds, remote location, and forgiving sand dunes. Crashes, design failures, and fierce weather challenged them at every turn. But they pressed on.

And then—history took flight.

On December 17, 1903, the Wright Flyer, a biplane powered by a modest 12-horsepower engine, rose into the air. Orville piloted the first flight, lasting 12 seconds and covering 120 feet, with Wilbur running alongside. That day, they made three more flights, the longest nearly a full minute. Today, markers trace the length of each historic flight. Natalie and Evelyn walked that same path at the Wright Brothers National Memorial, retracing the footsteps where human flight first began.

A Legacy That Soars

The Wright brothers' achievement at Kitty Hawk was not just a feat of engineering; it was a story of relentless perseverance. From a childhood toy to the world's first powered, controlled flight, they proved that vision, discipline, and grit could conquer even the most daunting frontier.

A visit to the Wright Brothers National Memorial reveals more than an invention; it shows their journey: the failures, the frustrations, and the unwavering belief that flight was possible. It's humbling to stand there and realize that in just 66 years, we went from 120 feet at Kitty Hawk to the surface of the moon. And today, we dream of Mars.

SMART TIP: The Wright brothers' story reminds us that the sky isn't the limit, it's only the beginning. When you visit Kitty Hawk, walk the very path where their dreams first took flight.

Tuscumbia, Alabama: Helen Keller and Coon Dogs

We had just hopped off our river cruise, bound for a place we had never even heard of, Tuscumbia, **Alabama**. When our bus pulled onto the main street, we gawked at the red-brick storefronts and graceful old homes. Where was the traffic? It felt like a Southern movie set, waiting for us to walk right in.

Sweet Home Alabama

Later, we'd explore the **Alabama** Music Hall of Fame, where legends like W. C. Handy, Nat King Cole, and Lionel Richie rose from their sweet Southern roots to global fame.

But first, we headed to a simple white clapboard house nestled among magnolias, honeysuckle, and boxwoods. This was Ivy Green, the birthplace of Helen Keller, born here on June 27, 1880. Her family owned a sprawling 640-acre plantation. Her father, a Confederate Army captain, settled here after the war, and the town itself had escaped much destruction.

Helen's childhood began like any other until tragedy struck when she was nineteen months old. An illness nearly took her life. She survived but was left blind and deaf. Her devastated parents, unsure how to cope, indulged her until she became almost uncontrollable. Salvation came when they sought the advice of Dr. Alexander Graham Bell (yes, the same Alexander Graham Bell who invented the telephone), who recommended a teacher: Annie Sullivan.

Annie and Helen

Annie arrived on March 3, 1887, and quickly realized she had to separate Helen from her overindulgent parents. She set up their own little world at Ivy Green and began teaching by spelling words into Helen's hand.

The breakthrough came at the water pump. Annie pumped cool water over Helen's hand while tapping out W-A-T-E-R into her palm. Helen suddenly understood that things had names. We stood at that very pump, touched its iron handle, and shivered in the July heat. In that instant, a child's world opened, and history shifted.

Within six months, Helen knew 625 words. By the age of ten, she had mastered Braille. By sixteen, she was able to speak well enough to attend preparatory school, and by 1904 she graduated from Radcliffe College cum laude. Annie remained by her side, interpreting lectures and guiding her.

The spoiled child became one of history's most remarkable women:

This humble water pump changed the course of history. It was here that Helen Keller first learned to communicate—unlocking her world and, in doing so, transforming countless lives beyond her own.

an author, lecturer, and advocate who traveled to more than 25 countries, met world leaders, and championed the blind and deaf. Many of her international gifts are displayed at Ivy Green, including a serene Japanese garden with a traditional lantern.

Inside, the museum rooms hold family furniture, personal mementos, Helen's Braille library, and her original Braille typewriter.

Keeping the Story Alive

Today, Ivy Green hosts a nationally recognized production of *The Miracle Worker* each summer from June to mid-July. Tuscumbia also celebrates the Helen Keller Festival every late June, one of the longest-running outdoor dramas in the USA.

Coon Dog Cemetery

Of course, no trip to Tuscumbia is complete without showcasing **Alabama**'s quirky culture and rural charm. On September 4, 1937, Key Underwood buried his faithful coon dog, Troop, at his old hunting camp. It was such a heartfelt act that others followed. Today, there are graves of more than 300 coon dogs from across the USA. Rest here in the world's only Coon Dog Cemetery. Their headstones, some funny, some tender, make this a must-see slice of Southern storytelling. The Coon Dog Cemetery was featured in the 2002 movie Sweet Home Alabama.

Stroll Through Southern Charm

Tuscumbia may be small, but it's bursting with character. From historic Ivy Green to parks and music, from red-brick storefronts to coon dog graves, this little town knows how to surprise.

SMART TIP: Plan your visit to Tuscumbia, **Alabama**, in late June to see the Helen Keller Festival and the outdoor production of *The Miracle Worker* at Ivy Green. This is a perfect blend of history and hometown pride. And don't skip the Coon Dog Cemetery; small, southern towns are full of human interest if you slow down and listen.

The Quiet Vermont Farm Boy
Who Became President

The Roaring Twenties! The Jazz Age!

It was a time of excitement and change in the USA: people danced the Charleston, watched silent movies, tuned in to the radio, made calls on newfangled telephones, and saw women win the right to vote. Airplanes took to the skies, prohibition sparked underground speakeasies, flappers challenged fashion norms, and baseball and jazz music captured the national imagination.

It was a raucous era of rapid growth and transformation.

And through it all, a quiet, unassuming man led the country; his name was Calvin Coolidge.

Plymouth Notch, Vermont

As we reached a small rocky hilltop, we came upon a cluster of white clapboard buildings that now make up the President Calvin Coolidge State Historic Site. The first structure we entered was the Florence Cilley General Store, once owned by the Coolidge family until 1917.

This peaceful place, Plymouth Notch, **Vermont**, is far removed from the roaring cities of the 1920s. Yet it was here that one of America's most understated but impactful leaders was born.

Born on the Fourth of July – A Real Yankee Doodle Dandy

Calvin Coolidge was born on July 4, 1872, an actual Independence Day baby. He grew up working hard on the family farm, studying diligently in a one-room schoolhouse, and developing a quiet strength that would one day carry him to the presidency.

We crossed a gravel road to visit the Coolidge homestead, preserved just as it was when young Calvin lived there. His childhood was marked by simplicity and self-discipline. Though he was not outgoing, his father saw promise in him and enrolled him in Black River Academy, several miles away.

There, Calvin remained reserved and didn't participate in sports, but he walked to the local library every day and read every book on the shelves.

Finding His Voice

Encouraged by his headmaster, Calvin applied to Amherst College in **Massachusetts**. At first, he felt like an outsider; the college's nine fraternities refused to accept him. But over time, he found a home in the debating society. He became one of the best debaters in his class, known for his clarity, logic, dry humor, and economy of words. His favorite subjects? History and politics.

From Plymouth Notch to the Presidency

After law school, Calvin slowly climbed the political ladder in **Massachusetts**: city council, mayor, state senator, lieutenant governor, and finally governor. There was no instant fame, just quiet determination.

In the 1920 election, he was selected as Warren Harding's running mate. They won by a landslide. But in 1923, President Harding died unexpectedly.

A Lamplight Oath – Silent Cal Takes the Helm

Coolidge was at home in Plymouth Notch when word came of Harding's death. That night, by the soft glow of a kerosene lamp, his father, then a notary public, swore him in as President of the United States. We stood in that very room, still filled with history and silence.

Coolidge remained true to his nature: thoughtful, measured, and famously brief. He earned the nickname "Silent Cal." One story tells of a woman who said, "I made a bet I could get you to say more than two words." His reply? "You lose."

But behind his silence was quiet strength. He made firm decisions, held to his principles, and believed in limited government, frugal spending, and the free market. Under his leadership, the economy grew rapidly.

A Private Man with Surprises

Though serious in public, Coolidge had a playful side. He adored his wife, Grace, and had a pet raccoon named Rebecca at the White House. He even exercised on a mechanical horse!

In 1928, he chose not to run again. He retired to write his autobiography and live a peaceful life. He died in 1933.

SMART TIP: When visiting presidential sites like Plymouth Notch, look beyond the politics, listen for the personality. Calvin Coolidge proves that strong leaders don't have to be loud. He stayed calm under pressure, spoke only when necessary, and let his actions do the talking. Sometimes, quiet strength leads to great success.

Mackinac Island:
The Guts to Persevere

Evelyn Kelly

No place is more beautiful in the summertime than **Michigan**. And no place is more fascinating than Mackinac Island. As for stories that changed the world, few are more compelling than the tale of Dr. William Beaumont and his window into the human body.

Michigan, the Great Lakes State, shaped like a mitten, is divided into the Lower Peninsula (the "mitten") and the Upper Peninsula (the "U.P."). Nestled between the two, covering only 4.35 square miles, lies Mackinac Island, whose Native American name means "Big Turtle." The only way to reach it is by ferry, and no cars are allowed.

I'm visiting my friend Mike, who lives in Caro, **Michigan**, on the "thumb" of the mitten. She insists I must experience Mackinac Island. Mike's infectious enthusiasm and knowledge of Michigan's hidden gems make her an invaluable companion on trips like this. Having her along ensures the journey is not just a sightseeing tour but a living, interactive adventure—she points out the nuances of local history, shares anecdotes, and helps me navigate the island like a true insider. I admit I mispronounced it at first: it's spelled "Mackinac" but pronounced "Mackinaw."

We park the car and board the ferry. We're not staying in the famous and elegant Grand Hotel, though we do visit it. Instead, we lodge comfortably at a quaint inn overlooking the main street.

History on the Bluff

The United States was barely out of infancy when Fort Mackinac was built on the bluffs of this island. On July 17, 1812, a combined force of British, Canadian, and Native American soldiers surprised and captured a small American garrison of fewer than 60 men. The British took the fort without firing a shot. But in 1815, after the War of 1812 ended, the fort was returned to the United States.

Today, it is a living history museum. Visitors can watch cannon firings and join reenactments. Mike, in fact, took part, defeating the "enemy" with theatrical flair. A reminder that history can be both educational and entertaining. Her participation brings the stories to life, showing that learning about history can be active, hands-on, and fun.

History comes alive on Mackinac Island from the thunder of a battle reenactment at the fort to the pioneering medical experiments of Dr. William Beaumont, where modern digestive science was born.

Dr. Beaumont and the Window to the Stomach

I am particularly drawn to the history of medicine. Imagine my thrill when I discovered that one of the most critical medical experiments in American history took place here on Mackinac Island.

Dr. William Beaumont, the son of a **Connecticut** farmer, apprenticed under a **Vermont** doctor, Truman Powell, as medical schools were scarce in his region. Beaumont served as an assistant surgeon during the War of 1812, later assigned to the remote Fort Mackinac, a hub for fur trading rather than warfare.

On June 6, 1822, a young French-Canadian fur trader, Alexis St. Martin, was accidentally shot in the stomach at close range. Beaumont treated him, expecting death, but St. Martin survived—living with a permanent hole in his abdomen. This unusual wound allowed Beaumont to observe digestion directly, inserting food on strings into St. Martin's stomach and testing gastric juices outside the body. He explored how temperature, physical activity, and even emotions affected digestion.

Though St. Martin initially grew weary of being a human guinea pig and ran off, Beaumont tracked him down and persuaded him to return. When Beaumont was reassigned to other posts, he took St. Martin along, continuing his experiments.

Why Beaumont and St. Martin Parted Ways

Despite their collaboration, Beaumont and St. Martin eventually went their separate ways due to a mix of personal and professional tensions. St. Martin grew increasingly frustrated with the invasive nature of the experiments and longed for a normal life free from constant observation. Beaumont, deeply committed to science, could not abandon his research. Their split was not acrimonious but inevitable: Beaumont went on to St. Louis to continue his medical career, while St. Martin returned to Canada to live quietly with his family. Yet, their unusual partnership permanently changed the field of medicine, proving digestion is a chemical process rather than a purely mechanical one.

Beaumont's groundbreaking work culminated in his 1833 publication, *Experiments and Observations on the Gastric Juice and the Physiology of Digestion*, cementing his reputation as the Father of Gastroenterology. His name endures in schools, hospitals, and even Beaumont Hill in Antarctica.

A Room Where Science Changed

Inside Fort Mackinac today, a small, unassuming room marks the site of Beaumont's experiments. Standing there, it's humbling to realize the magnitude of what happened in that quiet chamber, the secrets of digestion revealed for the first time.

Of course, such experiments would be considered unethical today. Yet it's important to understand the context of the early 1800s, when assumptions and norms were very different.

SMART TIP: Mackinac Island is more than car-free streets and famous fudge; it's where science, history, and beauty converge. Visit Fort Mackinac and step into the modest room where Dr. Beaumont's groundbreaking experiments changed medicine forever. Then slow down, bike, walk, or take a carriage ride to let the island's timeless charm work its magic.

Santa Fe: Turquoise, Desert Spirits, and an Artist

Turquoise Magic

Turquoise isn't just a beautiful stone; it's sacred. Native Americans used it in ceremonies and treasured it in jewelry. This blue-green gem, a mix of copper and aluminum phosphates, forms only in dry, barren regions with acidic groundwater. Its rarity made it prized from Ancient Egypt to Persia to China. In Santa Fe, every turn reminds you of its long-standing cultural significance.

Great Designs

We stumbled into the Santa Fe Indian Market, and turquoise was everywhere. Its presence seemed to embody the city's spirit, much like an Indian dancer adorned with ancient Navajo, Apache, Zuni, and Hopi designs. Here, tradition and artistry intertwine effortlessly.

Quirky Capital

Santa Fe's charm is hard to miss. The **New Mexico** State Capitol, or "Roundhouse," is unlike any other: a circular building inspired by the Zia sun symbol on the state flag. Forget portraits of politicians; walls display rotating exhibits of New Mexican artists.

Founded in 1610, Santa Fe is the oldest state capital in the U.S. It could claim to have existed before any on the East Coast. Its chili obsession is legendary. Adobe-style building codes are strict, even McDonald's looks like chili-dusted cookie dough. Legislators debate in cowboy boots, and the air hums with spicy energy.

The city layers history like a well-made enchilada. Long before the Spanish arrived, Pueblo peoples farmed corn, made clay pots, and built adobe homes. The Conquistadores brought Spanish traditions, and later settlers added their own touches. Today, Catholic cathedrals stand beside Pueblo kivas, and the sound of native drums mixes with guitars on the plaza.

Ghost Stories

We stayed in an old adobe hotel rumored to be haunted and heard tales of Ghost Ranch, an hour north. Known as *el Rancho de los Brujos*, the Ranch of the Witches, it's a desolate landscape of towering red cliffs, bleached cow skulls, and whispering winds. Some say cattle rustlers invented ghost stories to keep visitors away, but the eerie beauty speaks for itself.

Venture into the Navajo Nation to discover Canyon de Chelly, where Spider Woman once dwelled. This sacred canyon also witnessed the "Long Walk" of 1864, when the U.S. military forced the Navajo from their lands. Today, the Navajo are back, sharing their stories, and the canyon remains a hauntingly magical place.

Georgia O'Keeffe's Desert Stage

Near our hotel stood the Georgia O'Keeffe Museum, celebrating the visionary artist who fell in love with **New Mexico** in 1929. Born in **Wisconsin** and raised in **New York**, Georgia had never encountered a landscape like this. At Ghost Ranch, she found her studio, inspired not by ghosts but by bleached cow skulls, desert flowers, and cliffs that shifted color with the sun.

In 1949, O'Keeffe bought a home in Abiquiu, outside Santa Fe. Her house and studio became a sanctuary. The desert itself came alive in her paintings: massive red or white blooms, bones that symbolized endurance under the relentless sun, and the dramatic cliffs of Ghost Ranch and the Rio Grande Valley.

Visitors can even join the O'Keeffe scavenger hunt, spot a shape she might have painted, and become an official "junior Modernist."

SMART TIP: Santa Fe isn't a city to rush. Walk slowly and let your eyes drift across every mesa, canyon, and adobe wall. Start your day with a quiet stroll through the plaza at dawn, wander into a gallery or the Georgia O'Keeffe Museum while the morning is still cool, savor red chile at a local café, and end by watching the soft colors of the sunset.

Oshkosh, Wisconsin: Plane Fun and Adventure

Aviator, Margie Howard, with Evelyn

On the shores of Lake Winnebago sits Oshkosh, **Wisconsin**, a quiet Midwestern town that once a year transforms its airport into the busiest airport in the world. For one week every summer, the skies come alive as the AirVenture aviation event takes flight. The control tower handles more flights than Chicago O'Hare, Atlanta, and LAX combined. The locals beam with pride, knowing their small town has become the epicenter of aviation dreams.

Wisconsin AirVenture

We might never have discovered Oshkosh if not for our friend Margie. She and her husband, Gerry, were devoted aviators, so passionate that they lived on an air ranch where their plane could taxi right up to their front door.

For Margie, Oshkosh isn't just an event, it's a pilgrimage. During AirVenture, the fields transform into a shimmering sea of aircraft: ultralights, vintage warbirds, homebuilts, seaplanes, even balloons. In some years, more than 10,000 planes fill the runways and skies, creating the world's largest gathering of aviation enthusiasts.

When asked why she never misses it, Margie laughed, "Where to begin? Workshops, job fairs, museums, KidVenture for children, exhibits, demonstrations, evening programs on everything from aviation history to space. And then," she added with a twinkle, "there's still more."

Proud to be Different

At Oshkosh, even landings are unique. Except for emergencies, pilots skip the radio chatter and instead waggle their wings to signal acknowledgment from the tower. Colored dots painted on the runways allow multiple planes to land simultaneously, an aerial ballet of precision and trust.

And then there's the *FlyMarket*. Not a flea market but something more magical. Here you might find aviation antiques, quirky gadgets, souvenirs, or that one rare plane part someone's been hunting for decades. As evening falls, night air shows sparkle with pyrotechnics, drones, and aerobatic planes, twinkling against the dark sky like a constellation that has come to life.

More than an airshow, it's an aviation celebration. Evelyn's friend Margie soaks in the sights, sounds, and soul of Oshkosh, where thousands of planes descend on a small town each year.

Queen of the Skies

One year, Margie was thrilled to meet the family of Bessie Coleman at a booth for *Queen of the Skies*. Coleman, born in 1892, was the first African American and first Native American to earn a pilot's license. Known as "Queen Bess," she wowed crowds with daring stunts: loops, figure-eights, parachute jumps. She was called "the greatest woman flyer," though her life ended tragically on April 30, 1926, when a mechanic's forgotten wrench jammed her plane's controls in Jacksonville, **Florida**. Thrown from the cockpit, she died at just 34, but her legacy still soars.

Fall in Love with Oshkosh

For one week each summer, every day, Oshkosh becomes extraordinary. The skies buzz with noise, aerobatics, and excitement. Then, just as quickly, the town settles back into its quiet rhythm, waiting for the next season's love with flight.

SMART TIP: If aviation sparks your imagination, make Oshkosh in July a must on your travel list.

Moloka'i, Hawaii:
The Mule Train

By Valerie Gledhill, with Evelyn

Untouched by mass tourism and cookie-cutter high-rise hotels, the island of Moloka'i strives to preserve an authentic Hawaiian spirit. This island, known for its rugged cliffs and strong community, is home to one of the most poignant and touching events in U.S. history.

Our friend, Valerie Gledhill, shared this meaningful experience of her favorite place, Moloka'i.

A 1982 Excursion–Molokai

Our accommodation was a 6-unit condo right on the beach, with lots of entertaining crabs scuttling around. We were impressed by the local Chinese grocery store, which has exotic fruits and vegetables. However, although the beauty of the isle was terrific, our real adventure was in store: a ride on a mule to Kalaupapa.

Mule Train

As we gathered near the trailhead, high atop a cliff, a line of eager mules stood quietly, with twitching ears and alert eyes. I felt both fear and excitement. Here before me lay a trail descending more than 1700 feet to the ocean, and beside it were dense jungles and the world's tallest sea cliffs.

As my mule took his first step, I felt the ground move with the blue

Pacific in the background. However, the mule knew what he was doing and navigated with confidence. We clippity-clopped through 26 hairpin switchbacks. Scary!

I knew where we were going, Kalaupapa, a place not known for its beauty but for the sorrow, a leper colony.

I felt it. Riding where thousands of men, women, and children were forced down this path because they had Hansen's disease, also known as leprosy. These charming sea cliffs would become their prison walls; they would never leave.

At the bottom is the former leprosy settlement, established in the 1860s. Over 8000 people were sent there until 1969, when quarantine laws were finally lifted. That mule ride was more than a descent down a cliff. It was a passage into a deeper understanding of resilience, compassion, and the human spirit.

We arrived at the settlement. The mules sped up once they saw the beach and food.

I went to Kalaupapa for the adventure. I left with reverence.

Visiting the Settlement

We were introduced to our guide, a native resident who took great pride in discussing his small hometown. He asserted that he still lived there and had no intention of leaving. Philomena, a small church, stood there with weathered gravestones emerging through the grass. This was the legacy of Father Damien, even though Father Damien's remains were sent back to Belgium.

Father Became One of Us

He shared the story of the selfless work of Father Damien (1840–1889), a Roman Catholic priest born in Belgium, who volunteered in 1873 to serve the leper colony. In the 19th century, leprosy spread fear among the Hawaiian population. The misunderstood disease was believed to be highly contagious and incurable. In response, the Hawaiian government instituted a strict policy of forced isolation on the rugged, remote peninsula of Kalaupapa. Those suspected of having the disease were banished there and left with minimal care.

Father became a farmer, priest, teacher, and builder. He stayed there working and living among them until his weak body succumbed to the disease. He had become one of them—not just in spirit, but in flesh.

The gracious guide never mentioned his disability. However, on our car's dashboard was a photograph of a handsome teenager in a cap and gown. It was his son, whom he had never seen in person. Immediately after his birth, the authorities took his son to the Big Island. His only contact was through the mail. Nevertheless, he was so proud and enjoyed taking our town groups to see the approximately 30 people who still lived there.

In the Halls of Congress

The story of Father Damien and the leper colony on Moloka'i is one of the most potent examples of selfless service and compassion in modern history. And standing in the Halls of Congress is a statue, not of a king or a president, but of a humble priest who represents **Hawaii.**

SMART TIP: You can still visit the colony, but you must have a permit and go there for educational ventures, not as a tourist with a camera. As of 2025, mule rides have been suspended. You can visit in a small plane or on a guided hiking tour.

The Case that Changed America and a Can of Pepsi

Evelyn with Dr. Kevin Singer

Linda Brown, a charming 9-year-old third-grader, loved school. But there was a problem. She had to walk through Topeka streets and then catch a bus to the segregated Monroe Elementary School, one mile away, while the white Sumner Elementary School sat only seven blocks from her home. Her father, Oliver Brown, a welder and assistant pastor, thought this was unfair. When he tried to enroll Linda in Sumner, the school board flatly denied her admission. That moment changed not just Linda's life, but the course of American history.

Separate but Equal?

Back in 1896, the Supreme Court's *Plessy v. Ferguson* decision had established the doctrine of "separate but equal," declaring that segregation did not violate the 14th Amendment's Equal Protection Clause. But Oliver Brown—and many others—saw the daily reality: separate was anything but equal.

A movement to challenge this doctrine had already begun in the 1930s, led by Charles Hamilton Houston, the brilliant legal strategist often called the "architect of civil rights litigation." His star student, Thurgood Marshall, would carry the torch. In 1951, the Topeka chapter of the NAACP filed a class action suit on behalf of local black families, with Brown's name placed first on the list of plaintiffs. The case would eventually bear his name.

Brown v. Board of Education

After years of legal battles, the Supreme Court delivered its unanimous ruling on May 17, 1954: segregation in public schools violated the Equal Protection Clause of the Fourteenth Amendment. *Brown v. Board of Education of Topeka* overturned *Plessy v. Ferguson* in the realm of education and became the landmark case that reshaped America's public schools.

Enter a Topeka Native

That same year, 1954, a boy named Kevin was born in Topeka. He grew up in an all-white neighborhood, where desegregation was happening slowly, often so gradually that as a kid who loved basketball, he barely noticed. Life took him far from **Kansas**—through graduate school, teaching, and eventually a doctorate. But years later, while working in **Pennsylvania**, Kevin decided it was time to return home.

He interviewed with two school boards, and fate brought him back to the very district he had once attended. The district had gained fame in the struggle for Civil Rights and had undergone dramatic changes. The school was known for its difficult placement and low test scores. However, Dr. Kevin Singer embraced the challenge, becoming superintendent of the Topeka Unified School District. He poured his energy into helping students thrive, earning respect from both the community and his colleagues.

And then, of all things, came a phone call from Pepsi Company to recognize his work and accomplishments in the District.

The Pepsi Can Story

Kevin tells it best:

"When I was superintendent in Topeka, Pepsi wanted to put my picture on a can. I wasn't thrilled. It reminded me too much of those old milk cartons with missing kids. *'Have you seen this superintendent?'* After several requests, I said yes, but only if students could join me. They agreed, and we added a grade school artist, a middle school musician, and a high school basketball player.

The four of us posed for the picture, and soon the Pepsi can became a hot commodity in Topeka. Everybody wanted one, or at least our moms did! Years later, I even heard updates about those students. The artist appeared in a family photo at her grandmother's retirement party, and the cellist joined me for lunch in Philadelphia, where he now resides. Life goes on, and our soda can pictures turn into sweet, ancient memories."

It was a fun honor, but what mattered most to Kevin was seeing students celebrated alongside him. The community embraced it, buying up cans as keepsakes of local pride.

And so, in a full-circle moment, the city that sparked the case that changed America also placed its superintendent and its students on a Pepsi can.

Brown v. Board of Education reshaped America. Years later, its ripple appeared in an unexpected place—on a Pepsi can honoring education, leadership, and the students who carry that promise forward.

Photo Credit: Dr. Kevin Singer

SMART TIP: When visiting Topeka, **Kansas**, stop by the Brown v. Board of Education National Historic Site. Standing inside the old Monroe Elementary School, you'll feel the weight of history and the hope it created. It's a reminder that even small acts of courage, like a father enrolling his daughter in a nearby school, can change a nation.

PART 4

Great Cities—Large and Small— that Define a Nation

Two worlds, both urban and rural, weave the tapestry that is America. The pulse of New York, Chicago, and Nashville beats with ambition, innovation, and diversity. Yet, to understand a nation's soul, you must wander through small cities, towns, and even villages. In places like Savannah, Spokane, or Cody, life slows to a rhythm that values connection, tradition, and neighborly care. Whether under skyscrapers or starlit skies, both the bustling cities and the quiet towns define who we are.

America's Big Cities: Their Contribution to the USA

For most of our lives, we've lived in small or medium-sized cities, places where traffic doesn't dictate your day, the news cycle is quieter, and the pace of life feels manageable. Yet every time we visit a major American city, we are struck with awe. The sheer energy jolts us out of provincial comfort and reminds us how vital these urban centers are to the nation's fabric.

We've chosen seven cities: New York, Chicago, Miami, Nashville, San Francisco, Washington, D.C., and Las Vegas. Of course, countless others could be named, but these seven stand out for the distinct "notes" they contribute to the great American symphony. Together, they reflect ideals of ambition, resilience, and imagination, hallmarks of a country that never stops reinventing itself.

New York City: Just a Small Bite of the Big Apple

Someone once said that Venice has more tourists than pigeons. If that's true, New York City is coming for the crown—its pigeons strut down sidewalks, perch on statues, and even ride the subway. Here we are in a city that truly feels like a world unto itself. Energy hums through every block, an electric current running beneath your feet. What should we do first—history, food, or entertainment? It's almost overwhelming. So, we made a plan, promising ourselves we'd go day and night, because after all, this city never sleeps.

Times Square. No visit is complete without diving into its neon dazzle—digital billboards, shoulder-to-shoulder crowds, and the buzz of nonstop excitement. And yes, this is Broadway Central. We couldn't resist seeing not one, but two shows.

Central Park. This oasis holds a special place in Natalie's heart. During her work travels, she often escaped here, perched on a bench with her laptop, watching ice skaters tumble, and small dogs chase squirrels twice their size. Despite the city's constant hum, the park remains a peaceful refuge. Bonus stops: the Central Park Zoo and the nearby museums.

Skyscrapers. The Empire State Building is iconic, so naturally, we queued up to ride to the top. What do we remember most? Not just the view, but the poor gentleman ahead of us with a tissue trailing from his shoe. We gently told him, everyone laughed, and it became one of those silly details you remember even more vividly than the skyline. Don't miss the Top of the Rock at Rockefeller Center, where the best part is looking back at the Empire State Building itself. And of course, we take selfies with the Chrysler Building, Grand Central, and Trump Tower.

Downtown. Downtown Manhattan is where America's past, present, and future collide. Rising above the skyline, One World Trade Center—known as the

Downtown Manhattan—where remembrance and renewal stand side by side, with One World Trade Center rising above the 9/11 Memorial, a place to pause, reflect, and remember those we lost.

Freedom Tower—stands as a moving symbol of renewal and hope. It's 1,776 feet of glass mirror both the shifting sky and the vibrant city below, where Wall Street meets the solemn quiet of the 9/11 Memorial. As we paused to pay our respects, Natalie reflected on her own memories of visiting the Twin Towers and of that horrific day. It was a reminder that even as the city rises, we remember. We shall never forget.

Museums. If you're a culture lover like we are, New York is paradise. The Metropolitan Museum of Art—one of the largest museums in the world—houses everything from Egyptian mummies to timeless masterpieces. Add the Museum of Modern Art and the American Museum of Natural History, a delight for both kids and adults. And with more than 170 museums across art, history, science, and architecture, choosing is half the fun. At a friend's suggestion, someone born and raised in the city, we added a museum to our list: the Museum of the City of New York, which beautifully tells the story of the city's people and neighborhoods. We've visited museums in London, Paris, and Florence—but nowhere compares to New York.

Neighborhoods. New York is a patchwork of five boroughs and hundreds of worlds. Chinatown's dim sum, Little Italy's old-world charm, and Greenwich Village's bohemian spirit, every corner feels like a new adventure.

This is just the tip of the Kellys' bucket list—a small bite of the Big Apple. But the real flavor of New York often comes from the stories you don't plan, the ones that find you when you least expect them.

New Visitors: A Subway by Any Other Name

Imagine seeing New York City for the first time, especially if you're from rural America: glass towers stretching to the horizon, crowded sidewalks flowing like rivers, the constant chorus of sirens and honking taxis. So much motion, noise, food, shopping: it's sensory overload in the best way.

Natalie's sister (and Evelyn's daughter), Sharlene, experienced this firsthand when she chaperoned a high school band trip from Jacksonville, **Florida**. After a long morning of sightseeing, the group set off in search of the perfect sandwich. They were determined to find a Subway shop.

She asked a passerby for directions to Subway. He pointed at the "Subway" sign. They all marched down the stairs only to find a concrete platform with trains. No sandwiches. She continued asking New Yorkers, and they continued guiding her downstairs, still no Subway.

Finally, she stopped a man heading down the stairs.

"Is there a Subway shop down there?" she asked.

He chuckled. "No, ma'am, but there is a subway train." Then, smiling, he added, "You're not from here, are you?"

That's when the lightbulb went on: in New York, "Subway" doesn't mean lunch. Laughing, she quipped, "No, we're from Mars."

SMART TIPS FOR FIRST-TIME VISITORS: Hop-on-hop-off bus tours are a great way to get your bearings. We rode one three times, and each loop felt brand new.

Always check your assumptions. A familiar word at home might mean something entirely different somewhere else. Travel reminds us to ask, observe, and laugh at ourselves along the way. And remember, NYC's mass transit system is called the "Subway."

Washington, D.C.: The Nation's Heartbeat

What does Washington, D.C., mean to the USA? It is not simply a city; it is the very heartbeat of a nation. Every dome, every monument, every flag fluttering in the breeze carries the steady rhythm of democracy. Unlike the capitals of old monarchies, filled with thrones and palaces, Washington was born from the ideals of freedom and equality. It is the capital of a bold experiment in self-government, conceived in the Enlightenment and entrusted to its people.

George Washington chose this swampy land along the Potomac to hold the heart of the Republic. French-born engineer Pierre L'Enfant drew plans not for castles but for wide boulevards and open spaces where citizens could gather. More than two centuries later, his vision still beats strong.

A City Like No Other

Washington is where the pulse of democracy can be felt most clearly. It is where laws are debated, justice is tested, and leaders are chosen. Crowds stream here in joy and sorrow, whether to celebrate victories, honor the fallen, or call for change. To walk these streets is to feel the throb of history and the steady cadence of hope.

For anyone who wants to know about America, Washington, D.C., is where the journey begins. It is here you hear the heartbeat of a nation: strong, steady, and enduring.

Where We Felt the Beat

When Natalie worked in Washington, lunch breaks were often turned into mini-history walks. She wandered the downtown streets, captivated by the city's storied past. Passing landmarks like the White House and Ford's Theater, where President Lincoln was shot.

Sites to see:

- **The National Mall** – America's front yard, where millions have gathered for marches, Fourth of July fireworks, and inaugurations. Natalie's sister, Sharlene, was in DC for her son, Aaron, who was marching in the National Mall in the presidential inaugural parade for George W. Bush in 2001. It was so cold that she was worried about Aaron's lips sticking to his trombone during the parade. She spotted the announcers' booth. Warmth. Shelter. Possibly coffee. So, she climbed the steps and knocked. The two men inside were wonderfully friendly. "**Florida**, huh?" they said. "Isn't that the place of the hanging chads?" (Yes, yes, thank you, America, we will never live that down.) Sharlene smiled and pretended not to care, because frankly, she was too busy thawing her fingers. They chatted when one of them asked, "Do you want my autograph?" Sharlene thought: Bless his heart, he thinks he's somebody. Out loud, she said, "Oh, no, thank you." He grinned. "I'm Meat Loaf." She almost snorted. Sure you are, and I'm the Queen of England." She laughed and said, "You mean Two Out of Three Ain't Bad, Meat Loaf?" "Yes," he replied, smiling. "That's me."

  Back on the Bus, the students were buzzing. "Did you hear? Meat Loaf is here! We'd do anything to meet him!" Sharlene just smiled and decided this little episode was going straight into the "things Mom never tells the kids" file until now.

Under the dome, democracy lives.

- **The U.S. Capitol** – Its dome gleams like a beacon at night, the heart of the chamber where laws are made, and voices converge.

- **The Library of Congress** – Over 173 million items rest here, including Thomas Jefferson's personal books.

- **The White House** – More than a home, it is the steady rhythm of leadership. You can take a tour of part of the White House by contacting your U.S. Representative. There are so many works to see, such as Gilbert Stuart's portrait of George Washington. It is famous because Dolly Madison rescued it during the War of 1812 when the British burned the White House. Natalie and I once stood outside the gates, watching visitors from around the world taking photos. Then we walked across the street to Ole Ebbitt Grill, where Ulysses Grant, Andrew Jackson, and Theodore Roosevelt are said to have refreshed themselves at the bar.

- **The Lincoln Memorial** – Lincoln gazes across the Reflecting Pool to the Washington Monument. We lingered here at dusk, listening to the echo of his words carved into stone, and felt his heartbeat for unity still resounding.

- **Arlington National Cemetery** – Across the Potomac, the silence slows the rhythm. Standing at the Tomb of the Unknown Soldier, we felt the heartbeat pause in reverence for those who gave everything.

- **The Washington Monument** – Rising like a heartbeat spire, it framed perfectly with cherry blossoms the day we visited, a living postcard of resilience and renewal.

- **Museums Beyond Count** – From the treasures of the Smithsonian to the secrets of the International Spy Museum, the pulse of curiosity beats in every hall. We always leave feeling more alive with wonder.

Unexpected Cameos in the Capital

When you're in D.C., just like Sharlene meeting Meat Loaf on the National Mall, you never know who might be sitting at the next table: the Speaker of the House, foreign dignitaries, or the occasional celebrity. Natalie was having dinner with her friend Clarence, a longtime D.C. lobbyist, when they noticed a camera crew filming two women nearby. They shrugged it off, focusing instead on their own lively conversation.

Six months later, Natalie's phone exploded with messages: she and Clarence had appeared in the background of a recent episode of *The Real Housewives of Orange County*, filmed during one cast member's visit to testify before Congress. In Washington, even an ordinary dinner can turn into an unexpected cameo.

SMART TIP: Because every step resounds with history, the city is best explored on foot. Since DC is large, visitors can use the Metro. It is convenient, user-friendly, and an easy way to reach destinations beyond walking distance.

Chicago: The City of Inventions, Pizza, and Pride

Look at what the wind blew in! Ask someone what they know about Chicago, and the first words you'll hear are *cold* and *windy*. People call it the "Windy City," but not because of the gusts sweeping off Lake Michigan. The nickname actually dates back to the 1800s, when visiting politicians were said to be full of hot air. Still, step off the L in February, and the icy blasts will stop you in your tracks—you might find yourself wishing for some of that political warmth.

Natalie's job took her to Chicago in mid-February. Even with four layers, the wind sliced through her coat like arrows. This Floridian had never felt such bone-deep cold. The wind is loud, sharp, and relentless, but there's one upside: you quickly understand why Chicagoans walk fast.

We begin our trip in the Chicago Loop, the city's central business district. Note: We said "began." We didn't get very far due to the numerous eateries, shops, theaters, parks, and sights to see. The name comes from the original cable car lines that formed a circle downtown. The L, or elevated train tracks, built in the 1890s, create a physical loop that encloses the area.

Out of the Ashes

In 1871, the myth was that Mrs. O'Leary's cow kicked over a lantern, setting the town ablaze. Instead of crying, the city rebuilt itself with magnificent buildings, thanks to famous architects like

Louis Sullivan, Frank Lloyd Wright, and Mies van der Rohe. By 1885, the world's first skyscraper, the Home Insurance Building, rose from the ashes.

Inventions and the City of Firsts

Chicago has many firsts in the American landscape. During the 1893 World's Fair, organizers promised visitors a thrilling ride in a spinning machine that took them 264 feet in the air, called a Ferris Wheel, and visitors loved it. The original is long gone, but its spirit lives on at Navy Pier, where kids and adults can still enjoy the ride. And copies of the wheel are in parks and fairs throughout the nation.

Chicago could be called a city of "firsts": the zipper, the dish washer (1893), the car radio (Motorola), mail order catalogs, deep-dish pizza (Pizzeria Uno in 1943), the vacuum cleaner, Cracker Jacks, the brownie (created by Bertha Palmer at the Palmer House in 1893), Twinkies (1930), the first nuclear chain reaction, and don't forget Playboy Magazine (Hugh Hefner, 1953).

Aerosol cans were around, but in 1947, a Chicago resident suggested filling one with paint, and voila, spray paint, an instant success.

Making travel easier, George Pullman, a Chicago engineer in 1862, came up with the idea for a luxury sleeping car for trains. At night, the seats unfolded to make sleeping berths. When he began mass-producing the sleeper, he also added innovations such as dining cars, lounge cars, and covered vestibules between cars. Other travel innovations included the car radio in 1930.

From Many, One

A tour of Chicago will take you to neighborhoods that are like their own small towns, but are part of the whole: Ukrainian Village, Pilsen, Chinatown, Little Italy—all celebrating their food and music from the old land.

Many immigrants were drawn to the booming industrial sectors and became part of the labor movement. They began demanding better wages, safer conditions, and fair treatment. Labor organizing led to the complex process of integrating immigrants into American life.

Chicago has so many sides and stories. It's a city that sings and loves sports. Natalie's favorite time of the year in Chicago is March 17, St Patrick's Day, when the Chicago River turns green. A modern highlight is Cloud Gate, a large, iconic public sculpture in Chicago's Millennium Park, known as "The Bean" because of its shape.

SMART TIP: Every American should visit Chicago. Although it may be called the second city compared to New York, it is first in ideas, innovations, and just plain living. But don't leave Chicago without eating deep pan pizza.

Nashville:
Old Boots, New Country

Nashville is more than a city; it's a stage where America discovers new sounds, looks, and ideas. Known as the "country music capital," its influence stretches far beyond fiddles and guitars into fashion, food, civil rights, and even politics.

The city's musical roots reach back to the 1920s when the Grand Ole Opry first hit the airwaves. While the trademark "Nashville twang" began in the hills of Appalachia, it was Nashville's powerful radio signal that pushed the sound into the national spotlight. Since then, legends like Hank Williams, Johnny Cash, and Dolly Parton have made the Opry, once housed in the old Ryman Auditorium, the beating heart of country music.

Nashville is more than a city—it's a stage where America discovers new sounds, looks, and ideas. We were excited to attend a performance where Charlie Daniels was honored in true Nashville style, with tributes from Trace Adkins, Eddie Montgomery, and Gretchen Wilson.

More Than Music: The Nashville Look

The Nashville sound is a rich blend: fiddle tunes from British settlers, gospel hymns from churches, and the haunting melodies of enslaved Africans. But music is just the beginning. Nashville is a magnet for songwriters, visual artists, and dreamers. Walk down Broadway, and you'll hear guitars spilling out of cafés, bars, and even street corners, each voice hoping to be the next star.

Fashion plays its part too. Think cowboy boots polished to perfection, rhinestone-studded jackets, and western hats that sparkle like stage lights. It's country chic, Nashville-style, with a swagger that's traveled far beyond **Tennessee.**

Tastes of Nashville

Of course, no trip to Music City is complete without its food trends. Southern staples like grits, ham, and collard greens hold their place, but Nashville has put its own fiery stamp on the culinary map with Nashville hot chicken, crispy, spicy, and unforgettable. Barbecue and pulled pork still rule the roost, and if you have a sweet tooth, don't miss a Goo Goo Cluster, a local invention of caramel, nuts, and milk chocolate dating back to 1912.

Nashville as a Civil Rights Trendsetter

Beyond music and food, Nashville has been a stage for justice. In 1960, young activists launched the lunch counter sit-ins here, sparking a movement that spread across the South. Future Congressman John Lewis became a leader in these very streets. Nashville proved that a city rooted in tradition could also lead the way in change.

Cultural Leader

History also sings in Nashville. A visit to the Hermitage, home of President Andrew Jackson, reveals both grandeur and complexity. The Belle Meade Plantation still tells stories through its dairy stables, carriage house, and preserved slave quarters.

And then there's the city's bold nickname: the "Athens of the South." It earned the title with its commitment to education and culture, capped by the full-scale replica of the Parthenon built for **Tennessee**'s Centennial. Inside stands a glittering 42-foot statue of Athena, taller than the original in Greece.

Education runs deep here. Nashville is home to sixteen colleges, including several noted Historically Black Colleges and Universities (HBCUs). In 1873, Cornelius "the Commodore" Vanderbilt endowed Vanderbilt University, hoping to heal a fractured nation after the Civil War and tie the South more closely to the rest of America.

Nashville Sets the Tempo

From fiery food to fiddles, rhinestones to revolutions, Nashville is not just keeping pace with the country; it's setting the beat. This heartland city is as bold and influential as any coastal hub, proving that trends don't always start in New York or Chicago. Sometimes, they begin right here, in Music City, U.S.A.

SMART TIP: One of Natalie's best friends lives in Nashville and recommends: start your day wandering Nashville's quirky shops and colorful murals, then catch a songwriter performing live at the Bluebird Cafe (book ahead, it fills up fast). Round out the evening with hot chicken from Hattie B's, and let a rooftop cocktail in The Gulch carry the sounds of live country tunes through the night.

Miami: A Latin Tapestry

Ask many outsiders, and they'll assume Miami is **Florida**'s capital. It isn't, Tallahassee holds that honor, but Miami claims something even larger: a role as America's cultural crossroads with Latin America. Music, cuisine, fashion, and style create a dazzling tapestry of influences. Amid the glitz, you'll still find old-timers who remember the Miami of decades past, reminding us how tradition and transformation coexist.

Every great romance has a little mystery, a little heat, and a lot of passion. For America, that romance is Miami. She is bold, colorful, and unapologetically quirky, the kind of partner who shows up in sequins for breakfast and insists you stay out dancing until sunrise.

If you're lucky, you might meet Miami's old families, the ones who pronounce it "Miama (uh)." They're rare now, but they remind us that before the crowd arrived, Miami already had charm.

Of course, Miami isn't just one city. She's a whole entourage: Miami Beach with pastel Art Deco, Coral Gables with Mediterranean poise, Coconut Grove with bohemian mystery. Together, they make up a dazzling character you can't quite pin down, which only makes her more alluring.

The Gateway

Before Fidel Castro's revolution in 1959, Miami's Cuban population was only about 10,000+. Then came the waves: Cubans fleeing, Haitians arriving with their rhythms, other Caribbean neighbors bringing their flavors.

Where to Go in Miami

If you want to understand why America keeps returning to Miami, it's because the city is equal parts mystery, heat, rhythm, and passion. Every neighborhood feels like its own little universe.

Little Havana – We strolled down Calle Ocho, where roosters strut like seasoned dancers and the air is rich with the scent of strong Cuban coffee. At Domino Park, Evelyn played dominoes with the locals while Natalie slipped into a salsa dance. We ended our visit with guava-and-cheese pastries at Versailles, a Little Havana staple.

We also visited Miami's new baseball stadium, known for its bold, modern design to reflect Miami's vibrant, tropical character. Built in 2012 on the historic site of the former Orange Bowl, the Presidents and legends stood on that field: John F. Kennedy once addressed the nation there. For Natalie, it's personal: her very first memory was celebrating the Fourth of July at the Orange Bowl, dazzled by fireworks long before she understood the stadium's history.

South Beach & Ocean Drive (Miami Beach) – Miami's most glamorous postcard: pastel Art Deco buildings, neon lights glowing after dark, vintage convertibles cruising by, and sun-drenched beachgoers adding to the scene.

Brickell – Miami's sleek financial district, full of chic restaurants, rooftop bars, and a fast-paced, modern vibe that feels like the city's heartbeat after dark.

Coral Gables – Known as "The City Beautiful," Coral Gables blends Mediterranean Revival architecture with lush, tree-lined boulevards and landmarks like the historic Biltmore Hotel.

Coconut Grove – Miami's bohemian whisper. Beneath banyan trees, cats wander the sidewalks like they own the place, and every boutique feels like a secret discovery.

SMART TIP: Visit Miami from November to April for pleasant weather. Avoid hurricane season (July through October). Visit beaches or popular spots early to avoid crowds. And end the day at sunset spots like rooftop bars in downtown Miami.

San Francisco: Shaping the West with Fog, Gold, and Quirky Charm

America has always had a wandering eye, gazing west with stars in its vision. Lewis and Clark got the first peek at the Pacific. Trails opened, wagons rolled — but not many people rushed in . . . until someone shouted the magic word: Gold!

1849: Gold! (And a Whole Lot of Dreamers)

Picture it: a sleepy coastal village of about 1,000 souls suddenly mobbed by tens of thousands chasing glitter in a pan. By 1850, San Francisco had become America's fastest-growing city, packed with miners, gamblers, merchants, and dreamers from China, Latin America, Europe, and the East Coast. Basically, it was the 19th-century version of *"going viral."* Everyone wanted in.

The hills rang with pickaxes, the docks overflowed with ships, and overnight, the town became a swirl of gold dust, ambition, and possibility. That restless spirit? It's still in the air today.

Quake, Fire, and the City That Wouldn't Quit

In 1906, the earth grumbled, and the city shook to its core. Fires roared through the rubble, leaving San Francisco in ashes. Opera star Enrico Caruso swore he'd never come back, but San Franciscans had other plans.

Their attitude? *"We'll rebuild. Better."*

And they did: bigger, stronger, and more stylish than before. A phoenix city, rising from the ashes in art deco, steel, and swagger.

The Bridge That Said "Oh, Yes We Can!"

Fast-forward to 1937: the birth of the Golden Gate Bridge, that fiery orange beauty stretching 1.7 miles across the bay where the Pacific crashes into the fog. Workers dangled from cables with minimal safety gear and maximum guts, finishing early and under budget. Today, the bridge stars on more postcards than any celebrity and still makes tourists brave the wind for that perfect photo.

An American icon in steel and sky—the Golden Gate Bridge.

Photo Credit: Ken Chatham

Silicon Valley: Where Ideas Print Money

Just down the road, another gold rush took hold, the digital kind. Garages became launchpads for billion-dollar dreams: Hewlett-Packard, Apple, Twitter, Uber, Airbnb, and more. San Francisco may have started with gold nuggets, but now it spins digital gold.

The City's Quirky, Lovable Side

Of course, the city's real magic lies in its quirks, those little details that make you grin, roll your eyes, or fall completely in love.

- **Cable Cars:** America's only moving landmarks. They clang, they climb, and sometimes stop mid-hill just to test your faith in gravity.
- **Sourdough Bread:** Tangy, chewy, and older than your great-grandparents. The original Gold Rush starter is still alive. Some people keep houseplants, and San Francisco keeps bread dough.
- **Chinatown:** The oldest in the USA, where dumplings taste like joy and red lanterns light up the streets.
- **Lombard Street:** Eight hairpin turns in a single block, like steering your car through a curly fry.
- **Painted Ladies:** Those pastel Victorian houses you've seen on postcards, framed perfectly by the city skyline (and *Full House* reruns).
- **Ghirardelli Square:** Because no trip is complete without chocolate, and this one's been sweetening San Francisco since 1852.
- **Alcatraz:** A chilling ferry ride away, where you can almost hear Al Capone's ghost practicing his banjo.

Fog, Fashion, and Rookie Mistakes

On one of our visits, we made the rookie mistake of thinking, *It's California — it must be warm!*

Cue Karl the Fog (yes, the locals named him). He rolled in, icy and smug, as we shivered in our "light jackets." Lesson learned: dress in layers, even in July.

SMART TIP: Give yourself at least three days. Ride the clanging cable cars, break bread with sourdough, wave to Karl the Fog, zigzag down Lombard Street, and ferry out to Alcatraz. San Francisco doesn't just shape the West, it shapes your memories, blending history, humor, and just enough weirdness to keep you smiling long after you leave.

Las Vegas: What Happens in Vegas, Stays in Vegas?

Our first adventure in Las Vegas was the grand finale of an overland journey to the West. We had precisely one day, one night, and a flight at the unholy hour of 3:00 AM. In that short window, we caught the spirit of a city unlike any other. We couldn't leave it out of our catalog of places that make a difference. New York may give us a foundation. Chicago lends us resilience and labor movements. But Las Vegas? Vegas is the glitzy dreamer, defying both desert sand and rattlesnakes with neon swagger.

Once There Was a Desert

The Mojave Desert is a forbidding stage with creosote bushes, rattlesnakes, and endless mirages. Mexican explorers, perhaps dazzled by a few patches of green, called the place *Las Vegas*, "The Meadows."

A dusty railroad stop appeared here in 1905. Then came the Hoover Dam in 1931, dragging thousands of workers to the middle of nowhere. Workers wanted something to do besides bake in the sun, and conveniently, that same year, **Nevada** legalized gambling. The neon era had found its canvas.

The Flamingo Hotel

We checked into the Hotel, unaware we were bedding down in a piece of mobster folklore. We only noticed the pink décor, flashing lights, and endless games.

Later, we learned its backstory. Billy Wilkerson dreamed of a posh resort but ran into trouble. Enter Benjamin "Bugsy" Siegel, who turned the dream into a luxurious casino-hotel, opening on December 26, 1946. This was the Mob Era, where showgirls, slot machines, and high-stakes glamour took over the desert.

Bugsy didn't live to enjoy it. He was shot in 1947. Legend insists his ghost still struts around the Flamingo, forever trying to collect his winnings. We didn't meet him, but we slept with one wary eye open.

The Strip

We left our room and stepped into the blaze of the Strip. It was August, 101 degrees of dry heat. Sidewalk sprinklers misted us like wilted lettuce at the grocery store.

The Strip is a world tour in neon.

- Why fly to Venice when you can ride a gondola under a painted ceiling at the Venetian, with your gondolier belting "O Sole Mio"?
- Why pack a passport to Paris, when Las Vegas lets you ride to the top of the Eiffel Tower for a stunning Strip view?
- Why trek to Rome when Caesars Palace delivers columns, fountains, and more toga-draped opulence than Caesar himself enjoyed?
- Why book a Nile cruise when the Luxor's pyramid and Sphinx rise from the **Nevada** sand?

And just when we thought it couldn't get any stranger, we faced The Sphere, a 366-foot orb of LED wizardry blinking with giant eyeballs, planets, and landscapes.

Fremont Street

For a glimpse of "Old Vegas" before the mega-resorts, stroll down Fremont Street. Under its canopy of lights, street performers, flashing signs, and history collide. The Neon Museum revives the city's vintage glow, and the Mob Museum, once a federal courthouse, tells the story of law, order, and everything in between. We skipped it this time; spirits (ghosts, not alcohol) were calling elsewhere.

The Ghost Tour

Sleep? Not in this town. Even with a 3:00 AM flight, we couldn't resist the midnight ghost tour of Vegas's darker side.

- The MGM Grand whispers echo from the tragic 1980 fire that claimed 85 lives.
- The Luxor glows with tales of Egyptian curses and unlucky guests.
- And at the Mob Museum, you half expect Al Capone to bang the gavel himself.

Las Vegas may be a mirage in the desert, but it keeps flickering with life, laughter, and a little afterlife.

SMART TIPS FOR FIRST TIMERS: The desert is brutal in the summer. Spring and fall are ideal. Visit on weekdays when hotel prices drop dramatically from Sunday to Thursday.

SMART TIPS FROM A GAMBLING INSIDER: Set a gambling budget and quit when you are ahead. We use ATM's at banks and not at a casino, where the charges are higher. To save money on drinks, play slots first before ordering. Drinks will be served for free.

Tiny Towns: Small but Mighty

In our **Florida** county, we once had a little town with the oddball name of Zuber. For a while, Zuber was buzzing with sawmills and lumbermen, but over the years, folks drifted off, and the town became the punchline to a joke. Then one day, the road department quietly took down the sign—and just like that, Zuber was gone. Now it is the home of a zipline flying over the tops of trees and a former lime pit filled with turquoise water.

It's a reminder that small towns can vanish as quickly as they appear. But across the USA, there are still a few tough little places clinging to life with grit, humor, and a lot of neighborly spirit. We picked three of them, each officially "incorporated" and proudly listed in the 2020 census, showing that small is beautiful.

Scofield, Utah – Population 26

Perched at 7,733 feet in the high country of Carbon County, **Utah**, Scofield is the kind of place where the sky feels closer than the next grocery store. In its coal-mining heyday, the town boasted hotels, saloons, and enough bustle to make it feel like a boomtown. But in 1900, tragedy struck when an explosion claimed the lives of 200–250 miners. That sorrow still lingers.

Today, Scofield is quieter but no less proud. Families of miners still live here, ranchers run cattle, and outdoor lovers come to fish and hike near Scofield Reservoir. Each year, townsfolk gather at the cemetery to lay wreaths in memory of those who built (and lost) their lives here.

If you visit, be sure to bring hiking boots, a fishing pole, and patience for mountain weather. Snow lingers most of the year, so summer is the best time to soak in the history, the lake, and the high-altitude air that feels like a tonic for the soul.

Edge Hill, Georgia – Population 22

Edge Hill, **Georgia**, in Glascock County, is one of those blink-and-you'll-miss-it towns, but don't blink too fast. Incorporated in 1939, it has a population of teachers, farmers, and a town council that can practically fit around one kitchen table. Their slogan says it all: "Small Things Matter."

The town was named by Sara Madison Wilcher, a schoolteacher, who thought it resembled a place she remembered from her childhood in **Virginia**. Locals joke that here the mayor can shake hands with every citizen before breakfast.

Edge Hill's claim to fame is its size. Stop for a photo with the city limit sign, because how many places brag about being small on purpose? Around here, small isn't a problem; it's the whole personality.

Monowi, Nebraska – Population 1

Yes, you read that right. Population: one. And that one is Elsie Eiler, age 89, the last resident of Monowi. She's the mayor, the tax collector, the bartender, and the librarian. She even issued herself a liquor license so she could keep the tavern running.

Inside the tavern, the walls are covered with signed dollar bills from visitors who came from near and far to meet Elsie. Her burgers are legendary, and so is her hospitality. Out back, her late husband Rudy's 5,000-book library is still open to anyone who wanders through.

Monowi might be the tiniest incorporated town in America, but it's big in heart, and on **Nebraska**'s official highway map, it still gets its own dot.

Tiny but Mighty

From 20 people to just one, these little towns prove that being small doesn't mean being forgotten. They're full of stories, humor, grit, and a sense of community you can't measure by population.

SMART TIP: Next time you're road-tripping, take a detour off the main drag and wander into a town with a population sign that makes you do a double-take, like Hot Coffee, **Mississippi**. Who knows, you might find a burger joint, a century-old church, an antique store, or even a one-woman government keeping history alive.

**Next, we explore mid-sized cities, neither big nor small,
but rich in character and deeply woven into
the fabric of America's strength.**

Hannibal, Missouri:
In Love With Mark Twain

We first "met" Mark Twain on a cruise of the **Mississippi**. Of course, it wasn't the real Twain but an actor, yet he had studied the writer's demeanor and history so carefully that he seemed authentic. He even guided us on a tour of Hannibal, **Missouri**, the boyhood home of Samuel L. Clemens, better known as Mark Twain.

Over the years, we've chased Twain's footsteps across the country. In Virginia City, **Nevada**, we saw the plaque marking the spot where he once edited a newspaper. At Lake Tahoe, another plaque told the tale of the day he accidentally set fire to the woods. In Hartford, **Connecticut**, we admired his beautiful home, though there you mostly view it from the outside.

But Hannibal is different. It's not just plaques; it's a living, breathing stage where American literature comes alive. This picturesque river town, perched on the banks of the **Mississippi**, lets you step right into Twain's world. You can ride a riverboat, listen to the calliope whistle, and picture

Natalie shares a moment with a Mark Twain impersonator on the Mississippi River.

young Sam Clemens watching "Old Man River" roll on. His famous pen name even came from riverboat slang: "Mark Twain!" was the call that meant the water was safely two fathoms, about twelve feet, deep enough for a steamboat to pass without running aground.

Hannibal *is* the Story

This town doesn't just reenact history; it lives it. Every summer, Hannibal hosts National Tom Sawyer Days. Children wear straw hats, townspeople dress in 19th-century costumes, and frog-jumping contests bring to life "The Celebrated Jumping Frog of Calaveras County." You can almost see Tom dashing barefoot down Main Street.

Walk along the brick-lined streets, and scenes from *The Adventures of Tom Sawyer* and *Adventures of Huckleberry Finn* spring to mind. Outside Twain's boyhood home stands a little white picket fence, where Tom once convinced his friends that painting was the best game in town. During Tom Sawyer Days, visitors can join in the fence-painting fun.

Twain's boyhood home is now a museum filled with artifacts that echo his stories. Just across the way are the homes of Becky Thatcher and Huck Finn, neighbors who never really existed by this name, but certain people in the town were the prototypes of the characters.

Underground Adventures

For a cool detour, step into the Mark Twain Cave, the very one where Tom and Becky lost their way and where Injun Joe lurked in the shadows. With lantern light flickering on the walls, it's easy to imagine being right there with them, winding through narrow, twisting passages. You can imagine what would happen if the light went out, like in the story.

A Journey on the Raft

Hannibal also honors Jim, the unforgettable companion in *Adventures of Huckleberry Finn*. His story, of an enslaved man escaping a sale, intertwines with Huck's own flight from an abusive father. Their journey down the **Mississippi** on a makeshift raft is more than an adventure; it's a meditation on freedom, friendship, and the human spirit. Many consider it the most remarkable American novel.

The Spirit Lives On

As we left Hannibal, we almost felt Tom, Huck, and Becky tagging along, waving us goodbye as we climbed onto the bus. The spirit of Mark Twain, mischievous, wise, and timeless, lingered with us long after.

SMART TIP: Bring along a copy of the *Complete Works of Mark Twain*. Reading his wit and wisdom while standing in his hometown makes the stories sparkle even brighter. And if you can plan your trip during Tom Sawyer Days, all the better; it's the closest you'll come to stepping straight into a Twain novel.

Helen and Dahlonega: Bavarian Charm Meets Golden History

Question? Why go to Austria to see Bavarian culture when you can go to Helen, **Georgia**? OR, why go to the Yukon for gold when you can go to Dahlonega, **Georgia**?

You may not realize that you can do both in a visit to the North **Georgia** mountains. Here you find the Appalachian chain at its best, with many creeks, streams, ridges, and valleys. Helen and Dahlonega are only 25 miles apart; both lie in the famous gold belt.

A Fairytale Village in the Georgia Hills

Natalie and Evelyn turn the corner, and there it was, a Bavarian village. We had stepped into a storybook. Like something jumping out of a Cinderella fairy tale, gingerbread houses greeted us at every corner. Windows were adorned with red geraniums, and the Alpine-style roofs told us the houses could shed snow. We have seen all this before in Austria and Southern Germany, but we are not in Europe or any of the 89 countries we have experienced when traveling the world. We are in **Georgia**, USA, about 80 miles north of Atlanta.

Still amazed, we hobble down the cobblestone-like street to the historic Chattahoochee River, made famous by Sidney Lanier in "The Song of the Chattahoochee." That song could arise from a biergarten with an accordion playing a happy tune (never a sad tune). Balconies are fascinating; we wave to the people watching. The streets of the town are lined with shops, especially baker's, so we went in. Big choice: do we want apple strudel or Black Forest cake? We took both.

Helen Changes Clothes

In the summer, Helen greets us in bright colors and sunshine, but the people here tell us she changes well with the seasons.

In the fall, Helen is alive with color and golden beauty. In the Bavarian spirit, they have Oktoberfest with dancing, music, and age-old traditions from across the sea. Winter lights bring light and sparkle like shaking a snow globe with fascination. Wow! Spring provides dogwoods and wildflowers for her hair. In summer, those waterfalls of the Chattahoochee offer a special treat for tubers.

Dahlonega, Golden Neighbor

The year was 1828 when Benjamin Parks was out on a deer hunt and stumbled upon a gold-bearing rock. The story went viral, and by 1829, thousands of miners flocked to the **Georgia** hills in search of their fortune. Now the Dahlonega gold belt is a collection of historical mines and creek beds that extends across several counties in north **Georgia**.

Dahlonega is larger than Helen in both population and land area. Its population is 6,884 compared to 531 in Helen. The name comes from a Cherokee word meaning "Ycllowearth/gold."

Visitors can explore the Gold Museum, which is housed in the old courthouse, and take tours of historic mines like Consolidated Mine or Crisson Gold Mine for panning opportunities. Helen also offers trips that may be more family and tourist-friendly. There is also the Gold Rush Days festival, held the third weekend in October, featuring hundreds of art and craft vendors.

Christmas Festivals

Both towns host annual Christmas celebrations with a traditional, Bavarian-inspired atmosphere. Dahlonega emphasizes "old-fashioned charm" with conventional decor throughout the historic town square. Helen offers a more festive and creative "Lighting of the Village." Helen also hosts an annual Christkindlmarkt with handmade gifts, food, and treats. Dahlonega is more relaxed, traditional, and historic, while Helen is more unique and colorful. You can comfortably fit both towns in one day's outing.

SMART TIP: If planning the Oktoberfest or winter holidays, arrive early or consider going on weekdays for easier parking and fewer crowds. Comfortable shoes are a must. To savor local flavors, try bratwurst with German pastries in Helen, then switch to Southern cooking in Dahlonega.

Oh, Savannah!

This story begins from the point of view of an early settler.

Here I am in Savannah—a dream made real. As I walk these orderly squares, I remember arriving in 1733, exhausted from the Atlantic crossing yet filled with hope. I consider how James Oglethorpe selected his settlers, not through bold posters nailed to tavern walls, but through quiet conversations with those who knew the worthy yet poor and unfortunate. He worked with churches, charities, and individuals who believed in second chances. The churches became his messengers, and through them, we were called to Savannah.

Some of us—like me, in imagination—came as indentured servants. We signed contracts for four or seven years, trading our labor for passage, food, and shelter, and for the promise that when our service ended, the land might be ours. It was not freedom yet—but it was a future. We were chosen carefully, expected to work, to behave, to build something meant to last.

Thus began the colony of Savannah, a city that would thrive. Planters built a booming cotton trade and, eventually, brought in enslaved people to work the land. Though Oglethorpe opposed slavery, he ultimately gave in to the pressures of the time.

Fast Forward 80 Years: The Civil War

General William Tecumseh Sherman marched across **Georgia** with Savannah as his goal. On December 21, 1864, Savannah's mayor proposed surrender without a fight, on one condition: that Sherman's troops spare the homes and citizens. Sherman agreed and famously telegraphed President Lincoln:

"I beg to present you, as a Christmas gift, the city of Savannah."

Your Gift Today

Because of that surrender, many of Savannah's historic homes were preserved. Today, they stand beautifully restored, welcoming visitors from around the world.

Places to Visit:

- **The Armstrong House:** A stunning Italian Renaissance-style mansion, now home to Armstrong College. It was featured in the film *Cape Fear.*
- **The Mercer-Williams House:** Our personal favorite. This was the boyhood home of Johnny Mercer, who wrote "Moon River" about the local waterway. The house also gained fame in the book *Midnight in the Garden of Good and Evil.*
- **Flannery O'Connor's Childhood Home:** Discover memorabilia from the 1930s belonging to the Southern Gothic author, who lived here as a child.
- **Juliette Gordon Low's Home:** Founder of the Girl Scouts, her house is a stop on the local ghost tour. Our guide told of a child in 1860s attire seen on the staircase. When the tour ended, the woman beside me whispered, "I saw that child when I first walked in."

Dining at The Olde Pink House

This is where Southern charm meets culinary delight. We enjoyed barbecued ribs, fried okra, and warm cornbread slathered in butter.

Forsyth Park

Savannah's answer to New York's Central Park. Its grand fountain is modeled after one in Cuzco, Peru. The park's moss-draped trees and shaded pathways have appeared in films like Forrest Gump, adding to its cinematic charm.

Bonaventure Cemetery

Overlooking the river, this serene resting place is filled with ornate monuments and centuries-old live oak trees draped in Spanish moss.

Forsyth Park—Savannah's answer to Central Park, where a grand fountain inspired by Cuzco, moss-draped oaks, and shaded paths create a setting so cinematic it even starred in Forrest Gump.

One Last Note

If you're expecting grand antebellum mansions like those in Natchez, don't be disappointed; most of Savannah's historic homes were built before that style became popular.

SMART TIP: Taste your way through fried green tomatoes, shrimp and grits, pralines, and juicy **Georgia** peaches. And don't miss Leopold's Ice Cream, where every flavor comes from a secret family recipe passed down from the original Leopold Brothers. Download the GPSmyCity app for a self-guided walking tour, or hop on an Old Town Trolley for a narrated exploration. And in the evening, go on the ghost/haunted tour. Given Savannah's history, you will find a ghost on every corner.

Spokane: Where The Davenport Shines and Bing Sings

We had never heard of Spokane, Washington, until we took a river cruise that began there. What a surprise it turned out to be, a city that doesn't overwhelm you with the glitz of Las Vegas or the steel skyline of Seattle, but instead quietly finds a place in your heart. As soon as we checked into our hotel, we set out on a walking tour. Right in the middle of downtown, a waterfall tumbles into the Spokane River, winding its way past hotels, shops, and restaurants. The sound of rushing water is the heartbeat of this city.

The Grand Davenport: Spokane's Crown Jewel

The Davenport is not just a hotel; it's an experience. Natalie and I both agreed it was one of the highlights of our trip. This magnificent landmark opened in 1914, a jewel of marble and gold in what was then still a frontier city. It was the first hotel in America to offer air conditioning, central vacuuming, an elevator, and a private bathroom in every room.

Louis Davenport envisioned a place where timber, mining, and railroad businessmen could gather around glowing fireplaces (once wood-burning, now gas) to strike deals and swap stories. Above the central fireplace hangs a painting of the Nina, Pinta, and Santa Maria, part of the hotel's Spanish Renaissance inspiration. Throughout the hotel, themed rooms enchant visitors: the Grand Pennington Ballroom, the Elizabethan Room, and the Venetian-inspired Hall of Doges. Every corner whispers of elegance.

A Boy Named Bing

While the Davenport dazzled Spokane's elite, just a few blocks away, a boy named Harry Lillis Crosby was delivering newspapers. Young Harry loved music and played drums in a band called *The Musicaladers*. Neighbors recall how he whistled while he worked, his voice "clear as a bell."

He adored a comic strip called the *Bingville Bugle*. One day, a neighbor remarked that Harry resembled one of its characters and nicknamed him "Bingo." Before long, it was shortened to Bing.

Spokane is proud of its hometown star. Today, you can visit the Bing Crosby Theater, where his movies are still shown, or walk through his boyhood home, now next to the Gonzaga University campus, his alma mater. Bing never forgot Spokane, even after Hollywood made him a household name. Long before he crooned "White Christmas," he was a kid shining shoes, drumming with friends, and dreaming big. Later, when he returned, neighbors would see him strolling through town, attending Gonzaga events, or stopping by his old barber shop.

Inside the Davenport, you'll even find a Bing Crosby museum filled with memorabilia from his Spokane childhood to his golden Hollywood years.

Spokane's Magic

When we tell friends about Spokane, we always say: Eastern Washington feels very different from the Pacific coast. Stroll along the Spokane River and hum a Crosby tune: picture Bing and his siblings in their modest Gonzaga home. Imagine the sound of those waterfalls echoing downtown. Spokane has its quiet magic, a blend of frontier grit, timeless elegance, and one unforgettable crooner.

SMART TIP: Spokane epitomizes what is special about America. In one day, you can stand in the elegance of the Davenport Hotel, then wander along the riverbanks where a boy named Bing once dreamed.

St. Augustine: America's Oldest City

By Evelyn Kelly

"Come and meet me in St. Augustine at the Casa Monica Hotel," Natalie said. "I'll be tied up in meetings during the day, but after that, the city is ours."

I didn't need convincing. The very name, Casa Monica, sounded like romance wrapped in stone.

When I arrived, the hotel rose before me like a Moorish palace, its towers capped with red tiles and its arched windows glinting in the **Florida** sun. Built in 1888 of coquina and concrete, it had the kind of presence that seemed to hold its breath between centuries. I couldn't help but think of the people who once swept through its grand lobby, wealthy northerners, draped in silks and furs, escaping the snow.

Natalie met me in the lobby. "We are in room 411," she said mysteriously. "It has a reputation."

"A reputation?" I raised an eyebrow.

"Ghosts," she said, grinning.

The Old Soul with a Spanish Heart

The next morning, while Natalie conducted her meetings, I wandered out to discover the city.

The cobblestones of St. George Street felt uneven beneath my feet, worn smooth by centuries of travelers. On either side, coquina walls glowed warm in the sunlight, and from balconies above, cascades of bougainvillea spilled like ribbons of color. I peeked into courtyards where time seemed to linger, secret

The elegant Lightner Museum rises behind Pedro Menéndez de Avilés, founder of America's oldest city, which is an enduring reminder of Spanish roots, Gilded Age grandeur, and centuries of stories.

gardens with trickling fountains, where pirates once hid their spoils.

St. Augustine, founded in 1565, is older than Jamestown or Plymouth. It wears its years proudly, its history written into every stone. I felt that most keenly at the Castillo de San Marcos, the hulking fort that still guards the bay. Its coquina walls, porous and resilient, absorbed enemy cannon fire instead of breaking. But what stayed with me was the legend of a Spanish commander who discovered his wife's betrayal. Both she and her young soldier lover disappeared, and centuries later, two entwined skeletons were found sealed in the walls. Standing there, I swear the sea breeze carried a faint sound of soft weeping that could have been the wind.

Ghosts in the Spanish Moss

By evening, Natalie was free, and we set out on the town. Spanish moss swayed from the massive live oaks, and the air grew thick with stories.

At Tolomato Cemetery, we paused by the iron gates. Visitors had told of children darting among the graves, monks vanishing when approached, even a boy whose cries echoed from beneath the earth after he was buried alive. I shivered as we lingered there, the silence broken only by the rustle of leaves.

The lighthouse was no less haunting. "Two little girls," Natalie said quietly, "daughters of the keeper. They died when their play cart tipped over." As if on cue, the sound of distant giggles floated on the wind. I looked up at the tall white tower, and for a moment, I almost expected to see two shadows skipping up its spiral stairs.

And then, of course, there was the legendary Fountain of Youth. We drank from the spring, smiling at the thought of Ponce de León. Eternal life? Perhaps not. Fewer wrinkles on the face? No, that didn't work. But vitality? Laughter? Wonder? That much the water surely gave.

Gilded Age Splendor

No story of St. Augustine is complete without Henry Flagler, the man who built an empire of hotels. We wandered into what was once his crown jewel, the Ponce de León Hotel, now Flagler College. Inside, sunlight poured through Tiffany's stained glass, dancing across marble staircases where once only millionaires had tread.

Across the street stood another of his creations, the Alcazar Hotel, now the Lightner Museum. Its rooms brimmed with the odd and the marvelous: player pianos, crystal, and, our favorite, Rota the lion. Preserved behind glass, his face frozen mid-roar, Rota had once belonged to Winston Churchill. How this lion ended up in St. Augustine was anyone's guess, but here he stood, watching over a city already full of legends.

Room 411

At night, we returned to the Casa Monica. Our room 411 was quiet, yet the hotel whispered around us. The fourth floor is said to be alive with ghostly activity: children's footsteps racing through the hall, doors creaking open, televisions flicking on and off, shadows drifting across the ceiling.

We waited in the dim light, certain we'd catch a whisper or a flicker. Nothing. Three nights, zero ghosts.

"Figures," Natalie said. "The one time I *want* to be haunted, nobody shows up."

"Maybe they did," I said. "But even the ghosts knew better than to mess with us."

SMART TIP: St. Augustine isn't just a city to see; it's a city to feel. Between the cobblestones and the Spanish moss, the laughter and the legends, you don't just visit America's oldest city. You fall in love with it.

Pike's Peak and the Donkeys of Cripple Creek

Sometimes called *America's Mountain*, Pike's Peak looms large in both history and imagination. Now famous for the Pike's Peak International Hill Climb, this 14,115-foot summit inspired generations of westward-bound pioneers during the **Colorado** Gold Rush. The mountain rises near Colorado Springs, and today's travelers can drive to the top in a round-trip of 2–3 hours. But be warned—the road is steep, the switchbacks sharp, and the guardrails scarce, especially above the tree line. The peak was named for American explorer Zebulon Pike, though he himself never reached the summit.

In the summer of 1893, Wellesley professor Katherine Lee Bates did make it. Standing at the summit, she penned the words to *America the Beautiful*, later set to music by Samuel A. Ward's "Materna." That majestic hymn remains a tribute not only to the peak but to the promise of the land.

High in the Rockies

On the mountain's backside, at 9,500 feet, lies Cripple Creek, a town with a story as glittering as the gold that built it. Legend has it that the rush began in the 1800s when a prospector found gold. By 1890, prospectors poured in, launching the last great gold rush in America. More than 500 mines riddled the hills, and the town swelled to 10,000 people.

This was no ordinary mining camp. Imagine wagons creaking under heavy loads, ragtime tunes spilling from saloons, and gamblers crowding every table. Then came 1896, when fire destroyed much of the town. Undeterred, residents rebuilt in brick and stone, leaving behind a sturdy main street that still stands today. Cripple Creek also played a role in labor history; miners here struck early for the eight-hour workday.

The Human Story

The town was filled with characters. One of the most famous was Pearl DeVere, a flamboyant red-haired madam who ran the opulent "Old Homestead" brothel. With velvet wallpaper, $50 champagne, and carefully chosen company, it was legendary in its day. Pearl died young, at just 36, but her house survives as a museum.

Life in Cripple Creek was tough. Families scraped by with grit, women ran boarding houses, miners descended daily into dark shafts with candles and dynamite, and children played in dusty streets under the shadow of fortune and danger. Visitors today can descend 1,000 feet into the Mollie Kathleen Mine on a rattling lift, experiencing firsthand the narrow tunnels and precarious conditions of a miner's life.

It's Great to Be a Donkey in Cripple Creek

One thing makes Cripple Creek unlike any other mountain town: its donkeys. These long-eared descendants of the burros that once hauled ore now roam freely through the streets. Locals dote on them, tourists feed them, and every June, the town celebrates them with "Donkey Days," a festival of races, parades, and pure mountain merriment.

Ghosts and Gold

Like any self-respecting old mining town, Cripple Creek has its share of ghosts. The Imperial Hotel is said to be haunted, and the old jail still echoes with the sounds of unruly inmates. Evening ghost tours keep the legends alive, mixing mystery with the mountain air.

A Town of Grit and Charm

Cripple Creek is more than relics of gold and whispers of spirits. It's a living tribute to resilience, the brick and stone that replaced the ashes of fire, the donkeys still parading where miners once toiled, and the casinos that hum with a new kind of gamble.

SMART TIP: Be brave on the mountain roads. The climb may make your heart race, but Cripple Creek, with its donkeys, ghosts, and golden history, will reward the journey.

Mystic, Connecticut: Where Time and Tide Embrace

Mystic, **Connecticut**, isn't just a town; it's a mood, a melody played by the sea. Its very name, *Mystic*, feels enchanted, like a word you'd whisper at twilight. Derived from the Pequot word *missi-tuk*, meaning "great tidal river," the name carries centuries of tides and stories.

Mystic River

The first thing you notice is the water. The Mystic River weaves time together. Colonial shipbuilders once hammered planks along its banks, while today kayakers and sailors glide where schooners once ruled. At Mystic Seaport Museum, tall ships rise like cathedral spires, and the creak of wooden planks under your feet makes you believe that you've slipped back to the 1800s. Children chase seagulls on the wharf while shipwrights carefully restore boats, preserving the art of sailing into eternity.

Evelyn stands along the docks at Mystic Seaport Museum, framed by historic ships that preserve centuries of maritime history.

As we wandered the docks, a sudden gust of sea breeze caught our hair, and we laughed like children. We paused beside an old schooner, its sails furled, imagining the families who had built, sailed, and lived aboard her. Natalie pointed out the tiny carved figurehead, and I felt a pang of connection—here was history, not as a dusty exhibit, but as a living, breathing story.

Mystic Seaport Aquarium

Across town, the Mystic Aquarium brought another kind of magic. Beluga whales drifted like snowy clouds underwater, their faces surprisingly expressive. To stand before them is to feel small and awed, as though you've been granted a glimpse of some gentle guardian spirit of the sea.

Then there's Olde Mistick Village, a recreated 18th-century hamlet that invites you to stroll, shop, and linger. Wooden signs creak in the breeze, little bakeries tempt with the scent of warm cider doughnuts, and cobblestone lanes lead you to treasures. Natalie stopped to admire a hand-carved wooden toy, and Evelyn lingered by a shop selling sea glass jewelry. We both felt the same quiet thrill: a moment of joy stitched into the fabric of an old town.

Mystic Drawbridge

And of course, there's the Mystic Drawbridge, the heartbeat of the town. When the bridge lifts to let a sailboat through, everything pauses: cars stop, tourists gather, conversations hush. We watched as a white schooner glided past, the water sparkling in the afternoon sun, and we realized that, here, time yields to tide. Life itself bows to the river.

Mystic is more than sights—it's a feeling. It's the warmth of a chowder bowl on a crisp afternoon, the sound of gulls circling above, the laughter of children feeding ducks by the river. It's history, yes, but also romance, whimsy, and wonder. To visit Mystic is to be reminded that the best places are not just seen—they are felt.

SMART TIP: Fall is a perfect time to visit Mystic, for the town holds magic in every season, even in the winter when the winds howl.

Cody & Deadwood: Meet the Wild West

By Evelyn Kelly

Nothing excites the spirit quite like heading West. Natalie and I set out for two towns that still swagger with spurs, tall tales, and rowdy charm: Cody, **Wyoming**, and Deadwood, **South Dakota**. Outlaws, lawmen, saloon ghosts, and rodeo cowboys, welcome to the Wild West, where "yee-haw" is still a perfectly acceptable greeting.

Deadwood, South Dakota

A town called *Deadwood* is practically begging for ghosts, gambling, and gunfights, and it delivers. Back in 1876, when gold was discovered in the Black Hills, tents sprang up faster than prairie dogs, and with them came gamblers, miners, and more troublemakers than you could fit into a saloon.

Deadwood adored its guns, and using them on your enemy was considered both sport and social commentary. Today, you can join the fun as staged shootouts unfold on Main Street. Step on the wooden boardwalks, and you're half in 1876, half in the current year, where we went into a saloon to watch college football.

At Saloon No. 10, history took a deadly turn. Wild Bill Hickok, fresh in town with a reputation the size of **Texas,** sat down for a poker game and never got back up. He was shot in the back of the head, holding the now-famous "Dead Man's Hand": two aces and two eights.

And then there's Calamity Jane, the original party girl of the prairie. She could ride a horse straight through a saloon, sing louder than the piano, and shoot straighter than most of the men she drank with. She wore men's clothes, cracked dirty jokes, and earned her name by warning that anyone who messed with her "courted calamity." Legend has it she once chased Wild Bill's murderer with a meat cleaver, because why bother with a gun when the kitchen supplies will do? When she died, she was buried next to Wild Bill at Mount Moriah Cemetery, where the two still share top billing.

Naturally, a place this rowdy is crawling with ghost stories. Hotel guests report footsteps in empty halls, poker cards shuffle themselves, and phantom laughter rattles the bottles in saloons long after closing time. Deadwood, where checking into a hotel might come with a roommate you can't see.

Cody, Wyoming

If Deadwood was built on gold and grit, Cody was built on one man's ego, and we mean that in the best possible way. William F. "Buffalo Bill" Cody lived more lives than a cat: trapper, miner, Pony Express rider, buffalo hunter. Thanks to dime novelist Ned Buntline, his legend galloped far beyond the plains, turning him into the ultimate Wild West celebrity.

Buffalo Bill was a showman, salesman, and shameless promoter rolled into one. His Wild West Show featured sharpshooters, trick riders, and Native American performers, wowing audiences from New York to London (Queen Victoria herself was reportedly a fan and sent the wooden bar in the Irma Hotel as a gift). Never one to miss a marketing opportunity, he built the town of Cody as the perfect pit stop before Yellowstone. Naturally, he built himself a hotel, too, the Irma, named after his daughter, where staged shootouts still entertain visitors today. Because what's a hotel without a few bullets flying in the lobby?

The crown jewel of the town is the Buffalo Bill Center of the West, five museums under one roof. You'll find Native artifacts, cowboy art, grizzly bears, and Buffalo Bill's costumes so glitzy they could outshine Las Vegas. We lingered longest in the art galleries, staring at Western paintings that make you hear hoofbeats and smell campfire smoke.

SMART TIP: Don't miss the Buffalo Bill Center. It's like the Smithsonian of the Wild West, minus the long security line and with a whole lot more spurs.

PART 5

Quirky Things—Only in America

Every country has its oddities, but America seems to specialize in them. From the Dummy Mummy in Jackson, **Mississippi**, to an **Illinois** museum with Santa Anna's Artificial Leg, Americans celebrate the unusual with pride. These quirky places and traditions remind us that creativity, humor, and individuality are part of our national DNA. It is proof that adventure can be found in the most unexpected corners of the USA.

From Two Egg to Hell:
Towns That Make You Laugh and
Ask "Did I Read That Right?"

For years, we drove along I-10, always chuckling when we passed a sign for a little Jackson County, **Florida**, place called Two Egg. We wondered, what on earth were the founders thinking? But as we traveled across all 50 states, we discovered that America is not only "the Beautiful," but also a treasure chest of quirky town names tied to a legend, a bit of geography, or a moment in history.

NORTHEAST

Intercourse, Pennsylvania

In the 18th century, "intercourse" meant fellowship and social exchange. Today, this Amish town attracts curious visitors for reasons beyond its history.

SOUTH

Two Egg, Florida

During the Depression, money was scarce in this **Florida** Panhandle town. Farmers often bartered with eggs at the general store, with two eggs buying a box of snuff or other necessities. One day, someone joked, "This is a two-egg town." The name stuck.

Hot Coffee, Mississippi

In the 1800s, travelers heading to the Gulf Coast would stop at an inn where the coffee, brewed with pure spring water and molasses drippings, was legendary. Folks soon began calling the place simply "Hot Coffee."

Toad Suck, Arkansas

When the Arkansas River ran too low for navigation, boatmen would head to a local tavern and "suck on the bottle until they swelled up like toads." Hence the colorful name.

Monkey's Eyebrow, Kentucky

In this **Kentucky** hollow, the land's curve above the bend supposedly resembles a monkey's eyebrow, whatever that looks like.

Booger Hole, West Virginia

This Clay County hollow was the scene of violent feuds and ghost stories in the 19th century. Though some locals once tried to change the name, tourists loved it so much that it wouldn't disappear.

Looneyville, Texas

Named after early settler John Looney, this **Texas** town is the punchline of many jokes, but its residents take it in stride.

MIDWEST

Hell, Michigan

We first heard of Hell from a fellow traveler on a cruise. He asked, "Have you been to Hell?" He then nearly doubled over laughing. Sure enough, Hell exists near Ann Arbor and thrives on playful tourism, complete with T-shirts ("I've been to Hell") and a Hell Saloon.

Normal, Illinois

This town was named for the Illinois State Normal University, a 19th-century school dedicated to training teachers. To locals, "Normal" is perfectly normal.

WEST

Truth or Consequences, New Mexico

Once called Hot Springs, the town changed its name in 1950 after a popular radio quiz show challenged any town in America to adopt its title. Truth or Consequences accepted—and the name has stuck ever since.

Boring, Oregon

Founded by settler William Boring, the town has leaned into its name with humor. It even partnered with Dull, Scotland, to celebrate "Dull and Boring Day" every August.

SMART TIP: If you're on the road and see a town with a quirky name, stop. You may uncover a story worth sharing. Take a selfie with the town sign, chat with the locals, and you might just discover that America's humor is as wide as its highways.

Talkeetna: Alaska's Little Secret

Talkeetna, **Alaska,** is a town nestled at the gateway to Mt. McKinley (also called Denali). It's the kind of place where the unusual is perfectly normal. From Anchorage, we boarded a train that rolled past mountains, rivers, and forests until it delivered us to this quirky little town. We visited in August, when the days are endless, and the city is buzzing with visitors. Our first stop was Nagley's General Store, a Talkeetna institution that feels like stepping into both a museum and a neighbor's living room.

Mayor Stubbs: The Cat in Charge

No story about Talkeetna is complete without mentioning its most famous politician. In 1997, when no human candidates stepped up for mayor, the town elected Stubbs, a friendly red-orange tabby cat. Unlike human politicians, Stubbs had no scandals, no debates, and no broken promises. He attended ribbon cuttings, welcomed tourists, and generally ruled with whiskered charm. For two decades, he was the heart of Talkeetna until, sadly, a dog attack in 2017, and he passed away years later. The town never formally elected a successor, but his kitten, Aurora, is now the honorary mayor.

The Moose Dropping Festival

If you thought electing a cat was quirky, just wait. For nearly four decades, Talkeetna's biggest claim to fame was the Moose Dropping

Festival. Here's how it worked: locals collected actual moose droppings and launched them from a height. Tourists and residents alike placed bets on where they'd land. Wacky? Absolutely. Popular? You bet. It was the highlight of summer until 2009, when overcrowding got out of hand, and the festival was canceled after a tragic accident. Today, the raffle tradition still lives on. And just to be clear, no actual moose were dropped, only their leftovers.

Life in the Winter: Talkeetna Winterfest

Being Floridians, we had to ask: how do you survive winters that are dark, frigid, and seemingly endless? The locals grinned and told us about *Winterfest*. December in Talkeetna is anything but dull thanks to this month-long celebration. Some highlights:

- **The Bachelor Ball & Auction** – Held the first Saturday in December, eligible bachelors are put up for bid, with winning bids sometimes climbing to $1,000. The prize? A dance and a drink at the ball.
- **The Parade of Lights** – Because it's always dark in December, the lights dazzle twice as much. Floats and costumes light up the first Friday of the festival.
- **The Wilderness Woman Contest** – No pageants here. Women compete by chopping wood, hauling water, and demonstrating true Alaskan grit. Winners may take home prizes like fur hats, rafting trips, or even a glittering gold nugget.
- **Ongoing Festivities** – Open houses, bazaars, gift shows, and variety performances keep the town glowing all season long.

Gateway to Mt. McKinley

Of course, Talkeetna isn't just about quirky traditions. It's also the official jumping-off point for Mt. McKinley. Climbers stop here to gear up and get advice before tackling North America's tallest mountain. For those of us who prefer adventure without the exertion, there are spectacular flightseeing tours over glaciers, river rafting excursions, jet boat rides, and some of the best fishing **Alaska** has to offer.

Glass-domed and climbing north, the **Alaska** Railroad carries us toward Mount McKinley — with a delightfully quirky stop in Talkeetna to meet the town's famous cat mayor.

A Town With Personality

Walking downtown feels like wandering onto the set of an Old West movie, only quirkier. Wooden boardwalks lead past colorful shops selling everything from fine art to smoked salmon to hand-carved moose antlers. The vibe is part frontier, part festival, and entirely unforgettable. If towns had personalities, Talkeetna would be that lively friend who always tells the best stories.

SMART TIP: Many **Alaska** cruises include a side trip to Mt. McKinley. After docking, you'll board the train for an eight-hour ride to the very end of the line. Don't skip this Talkeetna. It's not just a gateway to the mountain; it's an essential piece of **Alaska**'s eccentric soul.

The Dummy Mummy of Mississippi

Jackson, the capital of **Mississippi**, is today a thriving and influential city. Yet, it still holds onto much of the charm and tradition of the Old South. Its most iconic building, the **Mississippi** State Capitol, boasts a remarkable feature: a shimmering gold-leaf dome, topped with a golden eagle.

But there's one object in **Mississippi**'s history that has, at times, outshone even that glittering dome: a mysterious and captivating figure from Egypt, a mummy.

The Tale of the Mummy

This curious story was shared with us by Barbara S., a fellow traveler. There are a few versions, but they all agree on one thing: this is a story of great human interest and Southern flair.

Barb was an elementary school student in Vicksburg. In the fifth grade, students took a special trip to Jackson to study **Mississippi** history, political strategy, and, best of all, to see what they believed was a real Egyptian mummy. The anticipation was immense. Wide-eyed students would stand in hushed reverence, staring at the ancient woman, encased in linen, and wonder what her life had been like centuries ago.

From the Nile to the Delta

In 1924, spirits were low in Jackson. The South was still recovering from the Civil War and the hardships of Reconstruction. But nationally, interest in ancient Egypt had exploded after the discovery of King Tutankhamun's tomb. The treasures, the curses, the mystique. It was all the rage.

Seizing the moment, a state senator from Vicksburg, Thaddeus B. Quinn, decided to bring a bit of the Nile to **Mississippi**. He journeyed to Cairo and returned with a sarcophagus said to contain the mummified remains of a lesser-known princess from the Temple of Bastet.

She was slender, wrapped in ancient, cracking linen, and she became a sensation. For decades, from the 1920s through the 1950s, she was known as "The Lady of the Delta." Visitors flocked to see her, from schoolchildren on field trips to churchgoers on Sunday afternoons. Some even claimed the mummy carried a curse. Capitol employees reported strange sounds and unexplained occurrences after dark, adding to the intrigue.

A Medical Student's Discovery

By the 1960s, interest in Egypt remained strong, particularly in academic circles. In 1967, a medical student at the University of Mississippi needed a project. And what better subject than the Capitol's own mummy?

As he carefully prepared her for an X-ray, he noticed something odd: a strip of newspaper, printed in German, was stuck to her back. Intrigued, the team gently lifted her and sent her through the scanner. The results? Not ancient organs or royal bones. Inside were shredded paper, sawdust, and miscellaneous animal bones.

The Lady of the Delta was no princess. She was a fake—a cleverly crafted dummy.

From Mystery to Merriment

What could have been an embarrassing discovery turned into a charming local legend. Mississippians took it in stride and with humor. Every Halloween, the so-called "Dummy Mummy" might still make an appearance, dusted off and displayed for a new generation of curious onlookers.

After all, she may not be real, but she's unforgettable.

SMART TIP: When history plays tricks, enjoy the tale anyway. The "Dummy Mummy of **Mississippi**" reminds us that even when the mystery unravels, the story lives on. When exploring small museums or quirky local exhibits, don't just look for facts; look for the folklore. Ask a guide what they've heard over the years. You might leave with tales so fun, you won't care whether it's true.

For those who would like to visit the mummy, the mummy is displayed at the Old Capitol Museum in Jackson for a limited time each year (particularly around October/Halloween). Admission is free.

Santa Anna's Leg: History on One Foot

Springfield, **Illinois**, the capital of the Prairie State, has beautiful stained-glass windows and statues honoring heroes from the past. It's the city where Abraham Lincoln rose to prominence, and visitors can tour his presidential library, walk through his home, and visit his final resting place in Oak Ridge Cemetery. Architecture enthusiasts can even explore the Dana-Thomas House, a Frank Lloyd Wright masterpiece from 1904.

But tucked away in the Illinois State Military Museum, just a few blocks from the Capitol's grandeur, lies an unexpected artifact that always sparks curiosity: the amputated artificial leg of General Antonio López de Santa Anna.

The Alamo and Santa Anna's Rise

General Santa Anna was a charismatic and controversial figure in 19th-century Mexico. He gained international fame in 1836 as the commander of the Mexican forces that besieged the Alamo in San Antonio, **Texas**. Although the battle ended with Santa Anna's victory, and all Texan defenders were killed, it ignited a fierce call for Texan independence: "Remember the Alamo!"

Later that year, Santa Anna was captured at the Battle of San Jacinto. Though he was eventually released and returned to Mexico, his dramatic career was only beginning.

The Pastry War and His First Lost Leg

In 1838, a strange conflict broke out: The Pastry War. A French pastry chef in Tacubaya claimed Mexican officers had looted his bakery. When the Mexican government refused to pay for the damage, France demanded reparations and launched a naval attack.

Santa Anna, now back in military control, rushed to defend Veracruz. Legend says he went into battle in his nightshirt, summoned straight from bed. During the fight on December 5, a cannonball shattered his leg. It had to be amputated below the knee. Always a showman, Santa Anna later buried the leg at his home in Veracruz. When he regained power, he had the leg dug up and reburied with an elaborate state funeral in Mexico City.

But two years later, as political tides shifted, mobs exhumed the leg again, this time dragging it through the streets in mockery.

The Prosthetic Leg and the U.S. War

During the Mexican-American War (1846–1848), Santa Anna, true to form, returned to power. Now fitted with a custom prosthetic leg made from cork, wood, and leather, topped with a black boot, he resumed his military command.

But in 1847, while having a meal near the Cerro Gordo battlefield, American troops launched a surprise attack. Santa Anna hurriedly fled on a mule, leaving behind bags of gold and his prosthetic leg. Soldiers from the 4th Illinois Infantry seized the limb and took it home as a war trophy.

A Political Cat with Many Lives

Santa Anna was remarkably resilient. He served as president of Mexico eleven times, each comeback more unlikely than the last. He was a political cat with far more than nine lives and a flair for drama that extended to every part of his story, including his leg.

Springfield's Unique Souvenir

Today, that very prosthetic leg is displayed in the **Illinois** State Military Museum. Meanwhile, the rest of General Santa Anna's remains are buried in Mexico City.

Both Mexico and **Texas** have requested the leg's return.

But **Illinois** has a firm response: No. The leg stays. It's their piece of history.

We Want the Leg

In the 1920s and 1940s, students at the University of Illinois attempted to liberate the leg, either as a prank or as a tradition, to display at a football game. They failed.

SMART TIP: When visiting Springfield, **Illinois**, set aside time for the State Military Museum. It is one of those you-won't-believe-it-until-you-see-it museums. The prosthetic leg of Santa Anna is displayed alongside Civil War artifacts and modern military gear. Read the display notes to track the leg's "footsteps" from battlefield to museum. Then walk a few blocks to the Old State Capitol and Lincoln's Home.

Route 66: The Mother Road

Ask almost anyone about their dream trip in the USA, and chances are they'll say, "I want to drive Route 66 from start to finish." This historic highway has become a symbol of American culture, optimism, and individualism.

First established in 1926, Route 66 stretched from the Midwest to **California**, carrying families, workers, dreamers, and adventurers westward. Today, it's less about getting from Point A to Point B and more about embracing the journey—quirky roadside attractions, neon-lit motels, and history lessons hidden behind every curve.

We haven't driven the whole route, but like many travelers, we've sampled sections and gathered stories from those who've made the entire "storybook" journey. Beginning in Chicago, **Illinois**, at the famous BEGIN sign on Adams Street, the road winds for about 2,448 miles through eight states and countless slices of Americana. Plan about two weeks if you want to savor it all.

Illinois

Why Chicago? In 1926, this bustling hub was the logical starting point for the nation's first federally planned highway system.

From here, the adventure begins with vintage diners and roadside oddities:

- **Gemini Giant** (Wilmington). A 438-pound fiberglass Muffler Man clutching a rocket, built in 1960 to cash in on America's space craze. He now looms over South Island Park.

- **Polk-a-Dot Drive-In** (Braidwood). Burgers with a side of nostalgia—Elvis, Marilyn Monroe, and Betty Boop statues included.

Missouri

- **Chain of Rocks Bridge** (St. Louis). Built in 1929, this unusual bridge makes a sharp 30-degree turn midway. Closed to cars but perfect for walkers.
- **World's Largest Rocking Chair** (Cuba/Fanning). Standing 42 feet tall, this welded steel structure was once the record holder. It is a great photo op, especially on "Picture on Rocker Day."
- **Red Oak ll** (near Carthage). A ghost town reborn as art, dreamed up by Lowell Davis with shops, historic buildings, and whimsical details.
- **66 Drive-In Theatre** (Carthage). A starlit night, a retro screen. What better way to time-travel?

Kansas

- **Cars on the Route** (Galena). A former gas station turned quirky stop with ties to the Cars movie and a glimpse of old Ozark Plateau life.

Oklahoma

- **Blue Whale of Catoosa.** An 80-foot smiling whale built as a family attraction, currently under renovation, but beloved.
- **Totem Pole Park** (Foyil). Home to the world's tallest totem pole, created by folk artist Ed Galloway. His carvings include tributes from Philippine service days and even a John F. Kennedy portrait.
- **Round Barn** (Arcadia). Over 100 years old, this rare round barn is a Route 66 icon.

- **The Will Rogers Archway** (Vinita) Perhaps one of the most visually memorable stops, this striking glass-and-steel bridge spans the highway for that "you're-in-the-heart-of-America" photo moment.

Along historic Route 66 in Vinita, the Hi-Way Cafe invites travelers to add their hometown stickers to a legendary 1963 Rambler—a tradition that earned a Guinness World Records title for the most stickers on a car.

Photo Credit: Vicki Duncan

Texas

- **Cadillac Ranch** (Amarillo). Ten Cadillacs buried nose-first in the desert—bring spray paint and leave your mark.
- **Leaning Tower of Texas** (Groom). A deliberately tilted water tower was built as a roadside stunt.
- **Midpoint Café** (Adrian, TX). Celebrate hitting the halfway point of the Mother Road.

New Mexico

- **Blue Swallow Motel** (Tucumcari). Neon signs, classic cars, and a 1930s vibe.
- **Clines Corners.** Souvenirs from turquoise jewelry to rubber tomahawks.
- **66 Diner** (Albuquerque). Chrome booths, jukeboxes, and killer milkshakes.

Arizona

- **Petrified Forest & Painted Desert.** A quick detour reveals ancient fossils and rainbow-colored landscapes.
- **Wigwam Motel** (Holbrook). Sleep in a concrete teepee, just like travelers did in 1937.
- **Meteor Crater** (near Winslow). A massive pit formed 50,000 years ago, still jaw-dropping.
- **Standin' on the Corner** (Winslow). A tribute to the Eagles' hit song, complete with a bronze guitarist and mural.

California

- **Elmer's Bottle Tree Ranch** (Oro Grande). Two acres of bottle "trees," decorated with everything from rakes to guitars to surfboards.
- **Wigwam Motel** (San Bernardino). Another teepee motel to complete the theme.
- **Route 66 Museum** (Victorville). Free exhibits showcase the road's history and culture.
- **Santa Monica Pier.** At last, the *End of the Trail* sign greets travelers with ocean breezes and carnival lights.

SMART TIP: Route 66 isn't a race; it's America's open-air museum. Follow those hand-painted signs to a diner with pie "just like Grandma's" and chat with locals who remember when Elvis stopped by. Download a Route 66 app or grab a paper map—yes, the old-fashioned kind—and circle every oddball attraction. And here's a fun game: bring along a stash of Route 66 stickers or postcards to trade with fellow travelers. After all, half the fun is collecting stories, not miles.

America's Different Voices: Bless Your Heart

You may grow up on the rocky coast of **Maine** or in the sunflower fields of **Kansas**. You may come from the lowlands of **Mississippi** or a small **Delaware** town. You are an American who speaks English, but when you visit a new region, you may still feel like you've stepped into another world. Accents, traditions, and values shape how we see ourselves and, too often, how we see one another. They can also feed stereotypes and misunderstandings.

Yet the divides are not as broad as they appear. Beneath it all, people share the same hopes and needs. Bridging these American sections means listening across landscapes, appreciating what each region has to offer, and recognizing that diversity of place is not a weakness, but a strength.

Most of us have had moments when we've thought, "*That's so strange.*" But learning about regional differences can spark respect and affection for the great patchwork of American culture.

Great Lakes and the Ocean

(Told by Mike Hile, native of Caro, **Michigan**)

The Great Lakes are a fabulous, true treasure. My freshman-year suitemate at Michigan State University was from **New Hampshire**. The first time I ever saw dental floss was in our dorm, thanks to her!

That spring break, I went home with her to **New Hampshire**. Her father was a superintendent, and her mother, a high school English teacher. One day, they both took time off work to show me New England, with the ocean being the highlight.

Her dad asked, "What do you think of the ocean, Mike?"

I answered honestly: "It looks just like the Great Lakes." And it did.

That night, my friend was upset. She explained that her parents had gone out of their way to share something special, and my reaction seemed dismissive. I apologized—I hadn't meant to offend. To me, it was simply true.

Later, in May, she visited my home in **Michigan**. I took her to Caseville, on Lake Huron. The first words out of her mouth were: "Oh my gosh, it looks just like the ocean!" Exactly.

North and South Meet

(Told by Sharlene, a **Florida** native)

Growing up in North Central **Florida**, with family roots in **Mississippi** and East **Tennessee**, I was steeped in Southern ways. But my first year at Florida State brought my first real taste of regional differences.

My roommate was from **New York**. One evening, I told her to "mash the button" to turn off the light. She froze. "Mash? You mash potatoes. What does that have to do with a light switch?"

Later, she suggested we go to a bagel shop. I blinked. "What's a bagel?"

She explained it was like a doughnut, only not sweet. I wrinkled my nose. Why bother if it wasn't sweet? We decided to get doughnuts instead.

We laughed a lot that year, at the words we used, the foods we loved, and the worlds we came from.

The West Comes to Florida

Years later, Evelyn's grandson brought his fiancée from Lake Tahoe, **Nevada**, home to meet the family in **Florida**. At dinner, we asked what to wear and what to pack for their April wedding.

She said, "Bring your snow coat."

We all looked at each other. *Snow coat?* We didn't even own snow coats—we barely had sweaters. We spent some time trying to figure out which piece of clothing in our closets might qualify.

As it turned out, the April wedding at Lake Tahoe was warm. We never used the "snow coats" we cobbled together.

The Quilt of a Nation

This is America's greatest secret: it is not a monolith, but a quilt. Stitched together from coast to coast, each patch is distinct—different foods, music, traditions, and ways of seeing the world.

SMART TIP: To appreciate this quilt, we must approach each square with curiosity, not judgment. When we do, we discover that what makes us different is exactly what binds us together.

Idaho: Light on People, Heavy on Fun

daho may be one of the nation's least populated states, and yes, you'll find the expected mix of snowcapped mountains, rushing whitewater rivers, and golden rolling farmland. But tucked among the natural wonders is another side of Idaho: quirky, surprising, and just plain fun. These are the kinds of stories you'll be sharing when you get back home.

Celebrate the Center of the Universe

In Wallace, **Idaho**, best known as the "Silver Capital of the World," residents will tell you they also live at the "Center of the Universe." In 2004, the mayor, nudged by locals in a bar, officially proclaimed it so, invoking the ancient Greek principle of probabilism: if something can't be disproved, then it must be true. A manhole cover in the middle of town marks the exact spot, and visitors snap selfies standing at the center of it all.

Wallace has other curiosities too. The Oasis Bordello Museum preserves a piece of the town's mining-era past. When it closed in 1988, everything, from the velvet couches to the costume jewelry, was left as it was. The museum now offers a candid look at the women who once worked there. Madame Ginger, its last owner, employed five to eight women at a time, with two-week rotations, mandatory doctor visits, and a strict 60/40 earnings split. The building remains frozen in time, giving visitors a peek into a secretive chapter of **Idaho** history.

The Museum of Clean – Pocatello

Only in **Idaho** could cleanliness become a full-blown cultural attraction. Founded by Don Aslett, author of 40 books on cleaning and dubbed the "King of Clean," the Museum of Clean is a six-story celebration of spotless living. Opened in 2011, it features artifacts such as a 1860s Daniel Hess carpet sweeper and a 1902 horse-drawn central vacuum.

The museum doesn't stop at scrubbing floors; it celebrates "clean" in every sense: clean language, clean politics, clean arteries, even clean jokes. Kids love the playful exhibits, like a vacuum "cut-out" that looks like it's sucking them inside. Quirky highlights include Van Gogh's *Starry Night* painted across a toilet seat and "Big Don," a towering 20-foot janitor sculpture who keeps watch.

Idaho Potato Museum – Blackfoot

What would Idaho be without potatoes? At the **Idaho** Potato Museum in Blackfoot, you'll be greeted by a giant baked potato sculpture before diving into the spud's surprising history. Exhibits include the world's largest potato chip, a collection of potato-related inventions, and, yes, potato ice cream. The museum, housed in a donated Union Pacific railway station, also offers family-friendly touches, like potato-themed video games.

Sleep Inside a Beagle – Cottonwood

For one of the quirkiest gift shops in America, visit the Dog Bark Park Inn. This gift shop is shaped like a giant beagle, and inside, guests find everything dog-themed, down to the artwork. Hundreds of wooden dogs carved by the inn's owners make it a tail-wagging roadside attraction that's been drawing smiles.

SMART TIP: Idaho may feel like the middle of nowhere, and that's exactly the point. If you're heading for the state's offbeat treasures, start by flying into Boise (BOI), the hub for southern adventures and potato pilgrimages. For the "Center of the Universe" in Wallace or the stunning lakes of Coeur d'Alene, your best bet is to fly into Spokane (GEG), just across the **Washington** line. If your trail leads to Blackfoot's Potato Museum or the Museum of Clean in Pocatello, land at Idaho Falls (IDA). And for the delightfully dog-shaped Dog Bark Park Inn in Cottonwood, you'll find Pullman–Moscow (PUW) a convenient little gateway. No matter where you land, expect big skies, open roads, and small towns with personalities larger than life.

Natchez Trace:
A 444-Mile Quirky Trail

Some quirky things happen only once, but here is an entire 444-mile road filled with strange history, mysterious happenings, and remarkable beauty, all rolled into one. Stretching from Nashville, **Tennessee**, to Natchez, **Mississippi**, the Natchez Trace Parkway encompasses ancient Native American sites, haunted places, Civil War battlefields, plantations, the birthplace of a famous singer, the deaths of famous explorers, wildlife encounters, and some of the most breathtaking foliage in the United States.

We're on the Natchez Trace Parkway, and we're about to see it all.

The Devil's Backbone

This ancient trace began as a Native American footpath, worn deep into the land from centuries of travel. It gained the nickname "The Devil's Backbone" because trudging barefoot left travelers weary, blistered, and sore. Later, wagons, oxen, and horses struggled just as much along its rutted, muddy course. And to top it off, swarms of mosquitoes were always waiting for a fresh feast.

Natchez to Port Gibson

Our journey begins in Natchez, a town where history lingers in the grand antebellum homes. When word spread that the Union army was approaching, townspeople struck a deal: surrender their guns without a fight in exchange for sparing their homes. The Union Navy agreed, and many of the mansions still stand today, open for tours.

Long before the cotton palaces, the Mississippian Indians built a sophisticated culture centered around maize farming. Near Natchez lies Emerald Mound, dating back to around 1400 AD. Covering eight football fields, it once held temples and

Dunleith mansion was built in 1855, known for its striking Greek Revival architecture with a full encircling colonnade — the only one of its kind in Mississippi.

ceremonial buildings. Walking here feels like stepping into another century.

Continuing along the Trace, we come to Mount Locust Inn, a "stand" from the 1780s. Travelers often had to share beds with strangers and chickens. Union soldiers thought it was too beautiful to destroy, so it survived the war. Today, we can imagine what it was like to dine on catfish before bedding down with unknown companions.

Port Gibson to Tupelo

The Sunken Trace Walk is one of the eeriest stops. Here, the path is literally sunken into the earth, carved by countless footsteps over centuries. To walk it is to follow in the ghostly steps of Native people, settlers, soldiers, slave traders, and even future presidents.

At French Camp, a French trader named Louis LeFleur set up shop in 1810. The Choctaw called the place "French Camp," and today it remains a rustic stop with a log inn, café, and school.

Then comes Tupelo, a modern city with one claim to global fame: the birthplace of Elvis Presley. His tiny two-room shack, now a museum, tells the story of his beginnings, a striking contrast to

Graceland in Memphis, **Tennessee**. Nearby, the church he attended has been moved so visitors can experience the gospel roots that shaped the King of Rock 'n' Roll.

Tupelo to Collinwood

This stretch brings more mysterious mounds, built by Native cultures that thrived here a thousand years ago. Archeologists marvel at the vast trade networks these people maintained, reaching far beyond the Mississippi Valley.

Not far away lies the grave of Meriwether Lewis, the famed explorer of the Lewis and Clark expedition. His 1809 death remains shrouded in mystery. Was it murder or suicide? Standing by his marker feels like standing in the middle of an unsolved detective novel.

History buffs can also detour to Civil War battlefields nearby. Or stop in Collinwood, a small, welcoming town of about 1,000 souls. Locals will gladly share their favorite Trace ghost stories, along with a plate of true Southern cooking.

Collinwood to Nashville

The final leg of the Trace is rich in nature. Black bears roam the forests, deer dart across the road, and wild turkeys strut in flocks. Driving north, we finally arrive in Nashville, feeling as if we've crossed not just 444 miles but 1,000 years of American history.

SMART TIPS: When driving the Natchez Trace:
- Drive slowly. The speed limit is 50 mph, partly to protect the abundant wildlife.
- Plan for gas. Stations are scarce on the parkway itself, though towns just off the road can provide fuel and plenty of pie and biscuits.
- Best season? Mid-October, when the Trace erupts in fall color.

North Dakota: Prairie Roots, Cultural Boots

North Dakota? Really? For many travelers, it's one of the last states to check off the list. Isn't it just a lot of flat prairie with a few buffalo? Not quite. This northern sibling, carved from Dakota Territory in 1889, surprises visitors with national parks, quirky roadside attractions, and a rich cultural history that makes it well worth the trip.

Fargo: Not Just a Movie

The Weather Channel once declared Fargo **America's Toughest Weather City**. Bitter winds off the Red River can freeze eyelashes in minutes. But instead of sulking, the city turns winter into a party with ice festivals, quirky art, and a sense of humor colder climates seem to breed.

Mini-Story: The Murals Talk Back

Walking downtown, we stopped to look at a mural of a Viking riding a hot dog. A passerby noticed my bewildered face and said, "Oh, that's normal here. Last week, they painted a cow in a tutu." Fargo doesn't try to be serious—it embraces the absurd.

Inside hotel elevators, you may hear accordion music. Whether it's charming or haunting depends on how many days you've been trapped inside by a blizzard.

The city's arts scene is impressive: the Plains Art Museum holds over 3,000 works by artists from Warhol to Dalí. A few miles away, Bonanzaville preserves 43 historic buildings in a living museum town, perfect for anyone who has ever wanted to time-travel, minus the "flux capacitor."

Grand Forks

Eighty miles north, Grand Forks is even colder, but what it lacks in warmth it makes up for in hockey. "The Ralph," officially the Ralph Engelstad Arena, is practically a cathedral for University of North Dakota fans.

The Hockey Baptism

A friend dragged us to a UND hockey game, and before we knew it, strangers were painting our cheeks green and white. "You're one of us now," they declared. In Grand Forks, hockey isn't a sport; it's a rite of passage.

Bismarck: A Capital Story

Named after Germany's "Iron Chancellor," Bismarck is a city shaped by German immigrants and fueled in modern times by oil.

When the original state Capitol burned in 1930, workers earning 30 cents an hour built a replacement during the Depression. The new Art Deco tower rises 19 stories, the tallest building in the state. On its grounds, the **North Dakota** Heritage Center walks you through the state's story, from dinosaurs that once roamed the plains to the German farmers who toiled them.

Mini-Story: The Tower of Power

We asked a local why their Capitol looked more like an office building than a dome. He grinned and said, "Because we're practical. Why make it round when you can make it tall?"

Quirky Stops and Open Horizons

- **Devils Lake** – Despite the sinister name, this is a peaceful retreat. Legends swirl here: spirits of the plains, hardy pioneers, and even UFOs flashing across the big Dakota sky.

Mini-Story – A fisherman swore he saw lights over the lake. "Aliens," he said. We nodded politely, then wondered if he meant extraterrestrials or just ice shacks lit up after too much schnapps.

- **Enchanted Highway** – A 32-mile stretch near Regent with giant scrap-metal sculptures: geese in flight, a 70-foot trout, pheasants, a deer crossing, and Teddy Roosevelt in a stagecoach. The grasshopper alone could terrify crops for miles.

Mini-Story – Standing beneath the trout, we looked so small we expected it to swallow me whole. A local winked and said, "Don't worry, he only eats tourists."

- **Frontier Village** (Jamestown) – A recreated pioneer town, complete with boardwalks, general stores, and enough nostalgia to make you grateful for modern plumbing.
- **International Peace Garden** – Straddling the Canadian border, this 2,300-acre garden is a living symbol of friendship. With its manicured grounds, lakes, and a floral clock that actually keeps time, it's proof that peace really can bloom, even in the northern prairie.

German Heritage

The Germans who settled here in the late 19th century brought their traditions of music, food, and community. Today, you'll find Oktoberfests, polka bands, and thigh-slapping folk dances that can turn even the shyest visitor into a stomping participant.

Polka Pressure

We tried to watch politely from the sidelines at a festival, but within minutes, a grandmother in a dirndl dragged Natalie into the circle. Natalie's feet were no match for her polka expertise. She just laughed and said, "Don't worry, you'll learn." Natalie didn't—but the food helped her forget.

SMART TIP: Pair **North Dakota** with **South Dakota** for a two-state adventure. Wander Theodore Roosevelt National Park's Badlands, then cross south to see Mount Rushmore and the Black Hills. Together, the Dakotas are a surprising mix of history, landscape, and roadside whimsy.

Bemidji, Minnesota: Where Paul Bunyan Braves the Cold

When Evelyn was in graduate school, she went home with a roommate from **Minnesota**. At a University of Minnesota basketball game, she met a big, tall, blond guy who said he was from Bemidji. He was broad-shouldered, with hands like baseball mitts, and she half-wondered if he'd split logs for practice before class.

She asked about Bemidji, and he grinned: "Coldest place you'll ever see, but it's worth it. That's where Paul Bunyan lives."

He invited her up to meet Paul, but she never made the trip. Instead, she kept up with Bemidji through its legendary weather reports. When **Florida** gets a cold snap, she still warns friends, "Hey, it's Bemidji weather." But even after all these years, she has yet to stand eye-to-eye with Paul himself.

Northern Minnesota Charm

Bemidji sits in the heart of the Northwoods. In summer, trails wind through forests, kayaks skim Lake Bemidji, and sunsets pour gold across the water. It's also the first city on the Mississippi River, where you can actually wade in at the humble little stream that grows into the mighty **Mississippi**.

But as beautiful as it is, the river isn't Bemidji's claim to fame. The real headline? A lumberjack so big he makes the **Mississippi** look like his garden hose.

Paul Bunyan and Babe

Paul Bunyan, according to the stories, was 63 ax-handles tall, so tall his footsteps shook snow off trees three counties over. His pancakes? Cooked on a frying pan the size of a football field, greased by cooks skating across it with bacon strapped to their boots.

Babe the Blue Ox matched him stride for stride. Forty-two ax-handles wide from horn to horn, Babe could drink a river for breakfast and polish off a hayfield for lunch. Together, they carved **Minnesota**'s 10,000 lakes (Lake Bemidji, naturally, shaped like Paul's boot), and cleared forests by tying axes to Babe's tail and letting him spin like a furry, blue tornado.

Meeting the Giants

Arrive in Bemidji today, and you will see Paul and Babe standing tall on the lakefront. Paul grips his shining ax, while Babe's wide eyes suggest he's ready for another round of forest clearing. Stand beside them, and even on your tiptoes, you won't reach Paul's kneecaps.

But Paul isn't just a statue here; he's everywhere. His name marks parks, trails, and shops. Paddle a kayak, and you can pose for a photo that makes it look like Paul is pushing you across the lake with an oar big enough to stir the ocean. Follow his "footprints" into downtown shops for fudge, steaming coffee, or a T-shirt that declares *I hugged Babe*.

Are You a Lumberjack?

In Bemidji, everyone gets a shot at lumberjack glory. You can try axe throwing, though be warned. Paul never loses. At the high school, the annual "Lumberjack Games" pit teams against each other in curling, bowling, darts, axe throwing, and cornhole. Even the college teams proudly call themselves *The Lumberjacks*.

SMART TIP: Visit northern **Minnesota** in the summer; it's stunningly beautiful, and you'll have the chance to finally meet Paul and Babe.

Salem and Sleepy Hollow: For the Love of Spooky Stories

When autumn drapes the land in amber leaves and crisp air, we crave stories that send a shiver down the spine. Two places answer that call perfectly: Salem, **Massachusetts**, and Sleepy Hollow, **New York**. These are the twin towns of shadows and stories, where history and legend walk hand in hand.

Salem: Real History That Haunts

Stepping off the train in Salem feels like slipping through time. Cobblestone streets whisper of 1692, when fear and suspicion gripped this quiet town. On the green commons, it's hard to reconcile the beauty before us with the chilling truth, witchcraft trials that ended with 20 lives lost, not in legend, but in fact.

Witches in colonial times were seen as dangerous, their healing and wisdom twisted into the devil's work. Feuds, disease, and crop failures often sparked accusations. What lingers is not only their tragic fate but the reminder of how fragile justice can be.

The Spirit of Salem

Salem embraces its past with both reverence and spectacle. At the Salem Witch Museum, the story unfolds in shadow and light. The Witch House, Judge Corwin's home, stands solemn, the last tangible witness to those trials. At the Peabody Essex Museum, art and history mingle, deepening the tale.

By October, the entire town transforms into a stage. Witches and ghouls fill the streets; ghost tours echo with legends; broom-decorating workshops and haunted shows stir a playful chill. After nightfall, the Salem Ghost Walk carries you past flickering lanterns and dark corners where whispers seem to linger still.

Sleepy Hollow: Where Legend Rides

Farther down the Hudson, Sleepy Hollow greets visitors with quiet charm wrapped in autumn magic. When we arrived in late October, the village was alive: pumpkins glowing, children parading with balloons, the air tingling with excitement. Yet beneath the festivity, shadows stirred, reminding us this was the setting for Washington Irving's immortal tale of Ichabod Crane and the Headless Horseman.

Among the quiet paths of Sleepy Hollow Cemetery rest Washington Irving and other figures who shaped America.

The Spirit of Sleepy Hollow

We wandered Sleepy Hollow Cemetery, where grand mausoleums and weathered stones guard Washington Irving, Andrew Carnegie, Walter P. Chrysler, and others who shaped American history. Just beyond lies the Old Dutch Church and its modest graveyard, the very one Irving wove into his ghostly story.

Here, history doesn't shout. It whispers. The chill isn't from staged theatrics but from the rustle of leaves, the toll of the church bell, and the thought that somewhere beyond the bend, a phantom rider might still thunder past.

Salem vs. Sleepy Hollow

Both towns are steeped in lore, yet their spirits differ.

- **Salem** is bold, theatrical, and bustling, perfect for those who want history mixed with festival flair.
- **Sleepy Hollow** is quiet, literary, and atmospheric, ideal for lovers of legend and those who prefer their chills subtle.

Salem hums with energy, lined with inns and restaurants ready for the October crowd. Sleepy Hollow is smaller, more intimate, and best savored with a slower pace.

Choosing Your Adventure

- Do you crave ghosts, spectacles, and lively festivals? Salem awaits.
- Do you long for whispered legends, old cemeteries, and timeless tales? Sleepy Hollow calls.

SMART TIP: Visit in October. In Salem and Sleepy Hollow, autumn's magic makes the experience unforgettable.

Eureka Springs, Arkansas: Jewel of the Ozarks

Why travel halfway around the world to Brazil to see Christ the Redeemer when you can visit the Christ of the Ozarks right here in the United States? Why fly to Oberammergau, Austria, for the Passion Play when Eureka Springs stages its own epic version every year?

Real Mountains that Impress

A friend once told me, "We drove through the Ozarks, and those were real mountains. I've never seen such beauty or such winding curves."

The Ozarks span five states, and though they're less famous than the Appalachians, they're quickly gaining recognition as a major destination and are breathtaking. The name itself is believed to come from the French *aux Arcs*, "to the arches, named for a landmark near a trading post, later transformed by settlers into "Ozarks."

The landscape is captivating: soft, rolling peaks blanketed in lush green. Spring bursts forth with redbuds and dogwoods, while autumn sets the hills ablaze with fiery maples, golden hickories, and bronze oaks. The Buffalo River, America's first national river, winds its way through this wilderness like a ribbon of silver.

Founded in the late 19th century, Eureka Springs drew visitors with its "miracle" waters, believed to cure a wide range of ailments, from colds to broken hearts. The wealthy built elaborate Victorian mansions on the steep hillsides, giving rise to its nickname: "The Victorian Village of the Ozarks."

But don't expect a sleepy historic town. Eureka Springs is delightfully quirky. Art galleries brim with sculptures that seem to watch you, street performers might juggle or pedal past on a unicycle, and the Crescent Hotel, built in 1886, has earned its title as "America's Most Haunted Hotel." Guests report phantom footsteps, doors opening on their own, and chilling encounters with ghosts. Each October, the town embraces its haunted side with a Halloween celebration that transforms it into a living storybook.

Why Go to Austria?

Why fly across the Atlantic when Eureka Springs stages The Great Passion Play, one of America's most beloved outdoor dramas?

Performed from May through early November, this sweeping production depicts the final week of Jesus' life—from Palm Sunday's triumphant entry to the crucifixion, resurrection, and ascension. The set is multilevel, the costumes elaborate, the sound effects immersive, and yes, live animals share the stage. Special performances are held on Good Friday and Easter Sunday.

Beyond the play, visitors can tour the recreated Holy Land, explore the Sacred Arts Museum and Bible Museum, watch intimate performances of parables, and even meet "David the Shepherd" (and his sheep).

Why Go to Rio?

High on Magnetic Mountain stands the Christ of the Ozarks, a striking statue that rises 65.5 feet into the sky, with arms outstretched 65 feet from fingertip to fingertip. Built in 1966, its minimalist design has little facial detail but enormous presence. For many visitors, it's a moment of awe that rivals its South American counterpart.

Eureka Springs is a town of contrasts: a history both real and ghostly, healing waters alongside quirky attractions, and natural beauty that rivals that of Europe. Its caves, hidden waterfalls, and mountain scenery remind us that you don't need to fly to Norway or Austria for wonder; it's right here in the Ozarks.

SMART TIP: Pair your trip with nearby Branson, **Missouri**, the self-proclaimed "Live Entertainment Capital of the World." Between Eureka's history and Branson's shows, you'll have an Ozarks itinerary that rivals any overseas adventure.

Sitka and Juneau:
Alaska's Odd Couple

By Evelyn Kelly

My assignment from a speaker's bureau was to visit Sitka, **Alaska**, to speak to a group of educators on the topic of *"Humor as Therapy."* I was thrilled to travel to such a faraway place, even if it meant changing planes several times to board Alaska Airlines. The plane was late. By the time I arrived, late to my own meeting, the group of about 25 educators was already sitting in a circle, laughing and swapping funny stories. They chuckled when I walked in and assured me, *"The airlines are always late."* I realized the therapy had already begun, and the best part was still ahead: touring this fascinating city.

Sitka: Russian Soul in the Paris of the Pacific

Long before Juneau became Alaska's capital, Sitka was the crown jewel of Russian America. It was here in 1867 that the U.S. purchased Alaska for $7.2 million. The story goes that during the handover ceremony, the Russian flag tangled on the pole, and soldiers had to climb up to yank it free, not precisely a dignified start to American rule.

In the 1800s, Sitka was dubbed the "Paris of the Pacific." The muddy boardwalks may have been a stretch for boulevards. Still, the Russian influence lingered: the onion-domed St. Michael's Cathedral, samovars steaming with tea, pickled fish recipes, and the echoes of Orthodox hymns. Today, Sitka still celebrates its blended heritage with Alaska's oldest music festival, where Native, Russian, and modern influences merge.

The Sitka National Historical Park is a treasure of towering totem poles carved with ravens, bears, and long-remembered legends. Locals insist ravens are more clever than tourists—some have figured out how to unzip backpacks for snacks. No surprise there; native Tlingit stories remind us it was Raven who created the world.

Juneau: A Gold Rush with No Roads In

In 1880, a Tlingit named Kowee guided prospectors Joe Juneau and Richard Harris to gold. The discovery sparked a boomtown with 58 saloons, drunken celebrations, and a rowdy reputation. Originally named "Harrisburg," locals soon voted to switch the name to Juneau, perhaps because it rolled off the tongue better.

Juneau is the only U.S. capital with no roads leading in or out. Hemmed in by water and mountains, it can only be reached by boat or plane. When Alaska moved the capital here in 1906, it was the largest town around, and Anchorage was still in its infancy. The Capitol building, completed in 1931, isn't crowned with a dome but does boast sleek marble columns, a kind of frontier elegance.

Adventure is never far from downtown. Just 20 minutes away lies the Mendenhall Glacier, a sparkling expanse perfect for hiking and photography. Along the harbor, you'll find a life-sized bronze humpback whale, leaping mid-arc as if frozen in time. For a quirky touch, there's the *Upside-Down House* perched on a hill, with flowers growing root-side up. And yes—if you encounter a bear while walking, don't panic, don't run, and definitely don't hand over your lunch.

Alaska's Odd Couple

Together, Sitka and Juneau are like Alaska's odd couple: one steeped in Russian heritage and legends of ravens, the other forged in a rowdy gold rush with glaciers at its doorstep. Both are accessible only by sea or air, and both are steeped in Tlingit tradition.

They may be different in personality, Sitka, a soulful blend of Old World charm, and Juneau, a bustling capital surrounded by wilderness, but each offers travelers a memorable slice of **Alaska**.

SMART TIP: When booking an **Alaska** tour, ensure that both Sitka and Juneau are included on the itinerary. Together, they'll give you a genuine taste of Alaska's character, history, and quirks.

PART 6

Food, Fun, and Festivities

The story of America is told in its food, fun, and celebrations. From smoky backyard barbecues to citywide parades, from small-town fairs to Thanksgiving feasts, every region brings its own flavor to the table. Making a great tapestry out of the foods from many countries has given the USA a unique outlook. The dishes we share, the music we dance to, and the sports events bring us together, revealing the spirit of community and joy that define this nation. In this section, we savor the tastes, sounds, and traditions that make America one big, ongoing celebration.

The Entrepreneur and a Jar of Jelly

Y ou may be a pioneer or an immigrant escaping the despots of the world. You may be a farm or factory worker who finds a better way to make things run, or an innovator who turns ideas into industry-leading products. Or you may be one of the many in 21st-century America who has lost a job, faced adversity, and decided to build a new life.

Such is the story of Suan Grant, a woman who embodies the American spirit.

Jars of Jelly, Jars of Grit

Suan carries Grant's Jellies wherever she goes. On a U.S. Department of Agriculture trade mission to Guadalajara, Mexico, her jars traveled with her, representing not just her business, but her story. Twice her creations have graced the cover of *Fancy Food & Culinary Products*, and she has won the Dallas Gourmet Gold Award.

But the jelly is only the surface. Behind every small jar is a tale of grit, courage, and entrepreneurship, the kind that has always defined America.

Jamaica: A Spark of Inspiration

In 1974, Suan, then a single mother of two, spotted an ad from Project Hope seeking professionals to lead a mission in Jamaica.

Thinking she wasn't qualified, she hesitated but applied anyway. Soon, she was in Montego Bay, immersed in the culture and enchanted by the island's flavors.

She discovered the Scotch Bonnet pepper, affectionately called Scotty Bons, Boabs Bonnets, Bonney Peppers, or Caribbean red peppers. In Jamaica, these fiery little peppers found their way into everything: salsas, jerk chicken, even jelly. And Suan? She fell in love.

Entrepreneur Suan Grant, with her famous pepper jellies, is proof that passion can turn purpose into something delicious. Natalie and Suan became friends while advocating for Alzheimer's awareness and caregivers, a shared mission that sparked a lasting friendship.

Fort Lauderdale: A New Life, A Hard Season

In Jamaica, she also fell in love with Jackie Grant, whom she later married. When political turmoil struck the island, Jackie moved his business to Fort Lauderdale, **Florida**. There, Suan volunteered in her community and made pepper jelly for friends and family.

But life took a painful turn when Jackie began to lose his memory and sense of time—Alzheimer's disease had become their new reality. Suan cared for him for eight years, dedicating herself not only to his care but also to advocating for research and support to combat the disease. Natalie, who worked for a national Alzheimer's organization, met Suan during her journey, and the two quickly formed a deep and lasting friendship.

Oklahoma City: Reinvention in a Red Jar

After Jackie's death, Suan moved to Oklahoma City, **Oklahoma**, to be near her family. At 60, with three decades away from the workforce, she found doors closed to her. Her friends urged her to sell her pepper jelly. At first, she dismissed the idea; it was just something she made for fun.

Then she heard about a workshop at Oklahoma State University's Food and Agricultural Products Center (FAPC) that trained food entrepreneurs in marketing, planning, and strategy. She signed up. That decision changed her life.

In February 2009, she brought her recipe to FAPC. They helped her scale it, design a business plan, and find a co-packer. Soon after, Suan's Foods was born. Today, her jelly is sold throughout **Oklahoma**, with plans to expand—a humble red jar that surprises every palate with its bold, Caribbean flavor.

A Pioneer Spirit in Every Jar

Suan's story is the story of America. Entrepreneurship isn't about fancy offices or vast capital—it's about vision, determination, and the courage to step beyond your comfort zone. From the "jelly lady" to the "soap guy," these small-scale creators carry forward the lineage of America's earliest pioneers, ordinary people building extraordinary things.

SMART TIP FOR DREAMERS: Want to feel the American entrepreneurial spirit for yourself? Visit a craft show, home show, or farmer's market. You'll find it alive in every booth and at every table. Or better yet, take Suan's own advice:

"Don't wait for the perfect moment. Start with what you have, right where you are. If I can build a business from a jelly jar, imagine what you can do with your dream."

Foodie Adventures on a Culinary Road Trip

Yes, we try to watch calories, but sometimes the pull of a regional dish is too strong to resist. To truly love America, you have to taste your way across it.

Northeast: Hearty Meals and Heritage

In New England, on a cold **Massachusetts** day, nothing warms our souls like a bowl of creamy clam chowder. In **Vermont**, spring means tapping maple trees for syrup so fresh it almost glows. In **Pennsylvania**, we find Philly cheesesteaks and Amish shoofly pie waiting on the table.

But nothing defines coastal New England like **Maine** lobster rolls. Picture Evelyn and Natalie on a weathered dock, the salty breeze blowing their hair, seagulls calling overhead. A golden split-top bun arrives, lightly toasted and filled with chilled lobster claw and knuckle meat, dressed with just the right amount of mayonnaise. Some versions add celery, herbs, or a squeeze of lemon.

Lobster was once considered "poor man's food," even served to prisoners or used as fertilizer. But by the 19th century, it had climbed the social ladder into fine dining. Today, lobster rolls capture not just the taste of the sea but the history and essence of **Maine** itself.

South: Flavor and Storytelling

The South is where food and storytelling go hand in hand. **Tennessee** smokes its barbecue low and slow, **Kentucky** serves up fried chicken with a secret twist, and **Georgia** plates peaches in every imaginable way. Along the coast, Low Country shrimp and grits tell their own tale of blended cultures.

But one treat truly defines New Orleans: beignets. These golden squares of fried dough dusted with powdered sugar are rooted in French tradition and shaped by Creole kitchens. The word "*beignet*" means "fritter," and when French colonists were forced to relocate to **Louisiana** in the 18th century, they brought the recipe with them. Fried until puffed and airy, they became a New Orleans icon.

Go to Café du Monde in the French Quarter, where they've been serving beignets since 1862, 24 hours a day. Just don't wear black, powdered sugar tells no secrets!

Pecan Pie: Mississippi's Sweetness

Few desserts embody the South like pecan pie. In **Mississippi**, where the warm climate and rich soil make pecans abundant, the pie is more than food; it's a tradition. Charles (husband and dad) grew up with a pecan tree in the backyard, like so many families. The recipe was simple and had been passed down through generations.

The Kelly Family Pecan Pie
(easy to remember: 1-1-1-1-4):

- 1 cup sugar
- 1 cup light Karo corn syrup
- 1 stick of butter
- 1 teaspoon vanilla (you may want more)
- 4 eggs
- Chopped pecans

Stir together, pour into a pie crust, and bake at 375 for 15 minutes and then at 350° for 30 minutes. Done—and delicious!

Hush Puppies

A true Southern side, hush puppies are golden balls of fried cornmeal batter with onion and buttermilk. Legend has it that hunters and fishermen tossed these to their barking dogs, saying, "Hush, puppy!" Others say mothers fed their children to quiet them until supper was ready. However they began, today they're crunchy, fluffy bites of Southern comfort.

Midwest: Farm Traditions

The Midwest is America's farm table. **Illinois** offers deep-dish pizza; **Michigan** tempts with cherry pie (don't miss cherry blossom season!); **Kansas** brings smoky ribs.

And then there's **Wisconsin**—the land of cheese curds. Fresh or fried, these squeaky nuggets are the happy accident of cheesemaking. German, Swiss, and Scandinavian immigrants transformed Wisconsin's lush pastures into America's DairyLand, producing over 600 cheeses. Curds, once just byproducts, took on a life of their own in the mid-20th century, showing up at fairs, pubs, and roadside stands. Today, there are even curd festivals, curd queens, and speed-eating contests.

Southwest: Bold and Spicy

Here, flavors are fiery, colorful, and rooted in Native and Mexican traditions. **Texas** serves chili and smoked brisket; **New Mexico** celebrates green chile stew and stacked enchiladas.

Navajo Tacos

One dish embodies both pain and pride: Navajo tacos. Built on fry bread and topped with ground beef, cheese, lettuce, and salsa, they originated during the Long Walk of the 1860s. Displaced from their land and given only flour, lard, sugar, and salt, Navajo women crafted fry bread for survival. Over time, it became the foundation for a new kind of taco, layered with resilience, culture, and flavor.

SMART TIP: To fully experience the love of America, you must eat your way across it. Every bite tells a story, every flavor connects you to a place, and every meal becomes part of the adventure. When you try new foods, step off your diet.

Candy, Cakes, and Cone-Sized Dreams: Your Sweet Tour Across the USA

From chocolate kingdoms to cupcake towers, America's sugary landmarks are sprinkled coast to coast. Loosen your belt and follow the trail of sweet adventures that turn every stop into a treat!

Chocolate Dreams

Natalie was in heaven in Hershey, **Pennsylvania**, the chocolate capital of the USA. At Hershey's Chocolate World, she rode a simulated factory tour that took her from cocoa bean to finished candy bar. She created her own candy bar at an interactive station and stayed at the historic Hotel Hershey, built by Milton Hershey in 1933. Walking down Chocolate Avenue that was lit by Hershey Kiss–shaped streetlights, she felt like she stepped into a fairy tale.

Lollipop, Lollipop

Some candy is just meant to be colossal. In San Francisco, **California**, See's Candies boasts the world's largest lollipop, identified by Guinness World Records, tipping the scales at over 7,000 pounds. Meanwhile, Forest Lake, **Minnesota**, showcases a giant lollipop mural, transforming the town into a real-life Candy Land.

Jelly Bean Royalty

Ever wondered where jelly beans came from? These colorful treats trace their roots to Turkish Delight and got their hard shell to survive shipping during the Civil War. At the Jelly Belly Factory in Fairfield, **California**, marvel at giant bean replicas, vibrant mosaics, and the world's largest jelly bean, nearly 7,000 pounds. President Reagan kept a jar on his desk (licorice was his favorite), and yes, astronauts even took them to space!

Cupcake Dreams

Cupcakes may be bite-sized, but some sculptures are anything but. In Queens, **New York,** at the Socrates Sculpture Park, a giant cupcake once towered over the skyline. Springfield, **Missouri**, celebrates a giant Candy Mama–inspired cupcake, crafted from fiberglass, resin, and steel. **California** went even bigger with a 31.5-foot tower made of 25,103 cupcakes! Detroit, **Michigan**, joined the fun with a 1,224-pound record-breaking cupcake. Both **California** and **Texas** have a Cupcake Festival, where oversized sweets steal the show.

Pie in the Sky

Americans love pies so much that some towns throw entire festivals in their honor:
- **Maine** Whoopie Pie Festival – once featuring a 1,062-pound creation.
- Moon Pie & RC Cola Festival, Bell Buckle, **Tennessee** – complete with a Moon Pie parade.
- **Arkansas** Pie Festival, Cherokee Village – tastings, races, and pie-throwing contests.
- **Florida** Key Lime Pie Festival – celebrating the state pie the last weekend of July on the Space Coast.

Natalie, Evelyn, and Sharlene in Maine proudly holding up their hard-won Whoopie pies. They are made of two soft, cake-like cookies (traditionally chocolate) sandwiching a creamy filling of vanilla marshmallow or buttercream.

Ice Cream That Never Melts

LeMars, **Iowa**, the "Ice Cream Capital of the World," is home to Blue Bunny ice cream and 50 whimsical cone sculptures scattered throughout town. Museums of Ice Cream also pop up in cities like Boston, Chicago, Miami, and New York for extra sweet adventures.

Bonus Treats

Sometimes the sweetest adventures are the ones that surprise you! From jaw-dropping candy canes to donuts that could double as rooftops, these quirky treats bring a little extra sugar and fun to your journey:

- Red Lodge, **Montana** – a 20-foot candy cane lights up the holidays.
- Los Angeles, **California** – the iconic rooftop giant donut has starred in films, TV, and commercials since 1952.
- Collegedale, **Tennessee** – Little Debbie Park features snack-shaped sculptures and family fun, including a zip line!

SMART TIP: Map your sugar-filled adventure so you don't miss iconic treats or sweet festivals. Pace yourself to savor each stop, from chocolate kingdoms in **Pennsylvania** to ice cream sculptures in **Iowa**. Many towns host interactive experiences, tastings, and parades perfect for turning your sweet tooth into a full-blown fun.

Fields of Dreams: How Sports Shape Us

It starts early—when little ones first taste the thrill of a last-minute touchdown, the joy of a home run soaring over the fence, or the applause echoing through a high school gym. It happened to the Kelly family as well, and it has been passed down through generations. Nothing has pulled us together quite like Friday-night football under the lights, the excitement of watching championship games on TV, or the little girls in our family proudly stepping up to bat in a neighborhood softball league.

Sports have become the threads that weave through the fabric of American culture. They teach us how to cheer wildly in victory, how to swallow the lump of defeat, and, most importantly, how to do both with dignity. From them, we learn life's big lessons disguised as games.

Baseball: *Take Me Out to the Ballgame*

In the 18th century, the English introduced a game to the colonies that involved hitting a round object. By the 19th century, America had made it its own, and baseball became our first great sweetheart.

With its slower pace and timeless rituals, baseball enchanted fans when the country needed something steady and unifying. By the late 1800s, the sport was firmly rooted, and the names Babe Ruth, Lou Gehrig, and Jackie Robinson became legends written into our collective memory.

Yet for all its storied history, the most actual magic of baseball can still be found at a T-ball field with five-year-olds. Baseball hasn't just endured, it has grown up with us, generation after generation.

Football: Passion with Marching Bands

The first game of American football, then called "gridiron", was played on November 6, 1869, between Princeton and Rutgers. Borrowing from soccer and rugby, it quickly developed into a game of grit, spectacle, and unmatched pageantry.

Today, nothing compares to the electricity of a college game day. Come with us to Tallahassee, **Florida**. The whole town hums with excitement as we weave past tents and tailgates, the air thick with the smoky sweetness of barbecue. The stadium roars as Chief Osceola rides onto the field on his horse, planting a flaming spear into the turf. The marching band strikes up the war chant, fans raise their arms for the Seminole chop, and suddenly, the contest feels

When Chief Osceola charges onto the field, the roar says it all—one of the most recognized and electrifying entrances in all of college football.

like more than a game—it's a ritual, a feast of spirit and sound. And this love affair is echoed every weekend in college towns across the country.

Basketball: Loud but Loving

When Evelyn was growing up, the neighborhood kids nailed a bushel basket to a pole and called it a basketball. They didn't need much more than a ball and an eager group of players; it was exciting, scrappy, and joyful.

The game was invented in December 1891 by Dr. James Naismith in Springfield, **Massachusetts**, who sought to create a less rough indoor sport for restless boys. What began with a peach basket quickly became one of America's fastest, flashiest loves.

Today, watching basketball, whether in a high school gym or at an NBA arena, is a dizzying show of speed, strategy, and soaring leaps. It's a love that thrives everywhere, from polished suburban courts to makeshift hoops in inner-city neighborhoods.

Sports, we love you more with every season. You've given us traditions, rivalries, friendships, and lessons that last far beyond the final whistle.

SMART TIP: Who's your favorite team? Look up their schedule, mark the dates, and plan your next game-day adventure.

So You Want to Be a Mermaid?

(As told by Cindy Perfico)

When Cindy Perfico of Jacksonville, **Florida,** spotted an article in the *Southwest Airlines* magazine about a mermaid camp, she knew instantly: *This is for me.* Cindy has always had a taste for the offbeat, the whimsical, and the adventurous. She immediately called her high school friend, another enthusiast of unusual experiences, and together they set this shimmering adventure in motion.

And what an adventure it was. If you think Navy SEAL training is tough, **Florida** offers something equally demanding, though far more enchanting: Mermaid Boot Camp at Weeki Wachee Springs. Can you hold your breath, flip your tail, and smile for adoring tourists, all at the same time?

An Old Florida Attraction

Weeki Wachee Springs is no ordinary swimming hole. A constant 74 degrees year-round, the springs rise from deep underground aquifers, sending millions of gallons of crystal-clear water surging into the open pool each day. Nestled north of Tampa along Highway 19, this natural wonder has been a stage for fantasy since 1947, when the first mermaids splashed onto the scene.

From then on, the Weeki Wachee mermaids became **Florida** legends. They performed gravity-defying underwater ballet, executed flawless hair flips, and even managed the quirky feat of eating bananas and drinking soda—all beneath the surface. Tourists have long marveled from the 400-seat theater carved into the limestone, where thick glass windows provide a portal into a shimmering aquatic world.

In the 1960s, the allure of the mermaids reached even Hollywood, **California**. Celebrities, including Elvis Presley, came to see the magic firsthand. Today, the tradition lives on through shows, camps, and the devoted "mermaid sisterhood," former performers who reunite to celebrate water ballet techniques, sequins, and making dreams come true.

Cindy Goes to Boot Camp

The camp lasts for three jam-packed, unforgettable days. On arrival, Cindy and her friend were greeted warmly, handed their schedules, and whisked into the behind-the-scenes world of Weeki Wachee. They learned the history of the springs, explored the facilities, and met some of the legendary "mermaids of yesteryear" who appeared on mid-century postcards.

Then came the training. The first rule? Relax and look graceful.

That sounds simple until you remember that you are submerged in 74-degree water, battling a current, hair flying into your face, and a steady blast of spring water up your nose. No matter what happens, the mantra is the same: smile, be serene, and never let the audience see you struggle.

Breath control is the heart of the training. Mermaids practice holding their breath for extended periods, surfacing with effortless poise. "Pretend you are completely in control," the instructors say. "Even when you're not." The smile is as much a part of the performance as the glittering costume.

Here Comes the Tail

No mermaid is complete without her tail. Cindy first slipped into her two-piece bathing suit, then wriggled into the tail while kneeling in the shallow water. The fabric shimmered with iridescent scales, but make no mistake, this was no lightweight costume. The tail is surprisingly heavy, restricting movement and making every flip and twirl a test of strength.

The instructors taught Cindy to undulate her tail gracefully, dolphin-style, to propel herself forward. At first, her legs felt like cement. But with practice, she learned to kick, twirl, and glide in unison with her fellow "trainees."

And then it was time to put it all together: breath control, graceful movement, synchronized performance, and above all, the mermaid smile.

A Spiritual Experience

When Cindy finally slipped beneath the surface in full costume, something extraordinary happened.

"You are weightless, like drifting in a dream," she said. "The light filtering down through the water is like stained-glass windows in a cathedral. Each bubble you release is silvery and slow, like time itself has paused. All the noise of the world disappears. It feels as if you're hovering between gravity and freedom—like you've entered another realm, something otherworldly, humbling, and profoundly spiritual."

Cindy Perfico lives a fantasy, becoming a mermaid in the crystal-clear waters of Weeki Wachee Springs, a magical, almost spiritual moment beneath the surface. Photo Credit: Cindy Perfico

For Cindy, those three days weren't about becoming a professional performer. They were about living a fantasy, experiencing something magical, and claiming a memory she'll treasure for life. "It was marvelous," she said. "The highlight of a lifetime."

So—Do You Still Want to Be a Mermaid?

If you're tempted, Mermaid Boot Camp might just be calling your name. Who knows—you might find yourself transformed, even if only for a weekend.

SMART TIP: As of 2025, Weeki Wachee offers a new magical experience, the *Mermaid Boutique.* Perfect for children (and children at heart), it provides enchanting mermaid makeovers complete with sparkling tails, glittering makeup, and a chance to feel part of this timeless **Florida** fantasy.

Voices Through the Airwaves: When Radio and Television Connected America

Let's Pretend

On Saturday morning, everything came to a halt when it was time for *Let's Pretend*. Evelyn had to be near the radio in the living room, ready to hear the story of the day.

She can still hear the jingle:

"Cream of Wheat is so good to eat – we have it every day.
We sing this song – it will make us strong,
And it makes us shout hurray!"

She sang along gleefully, then settled in for the fairy tales—*Cinderella, Sleeping Beauty*, and the one she enjoyed the most: *Rumpelstiltskin*.

Beloved Radio Programs

These dramatized stories, broadcast on CBS Radio from 1934 to 1954, brought wonder into our homes. With talented voice actors—both adults and children—paired with classical music and creative sound effects, the tales felt as vivid as any modern-day movie.

Before smartphones, the radio was a magical wooden box that brought the world to life. Evelyn credits those Saturdays spent with *Let's Pretend* for sparking both her love of storytelling and her longing to travel.

And Saturday wasn't the only day she tuned in. Each weekday, the *Lone Ranger and Tonto* whisked us away to the American Southwest with stories of justice and dusty deserts. She laughed at *Fibber McGee and Molly*, especially when that famous overstuffed closet spilled out its contents—so iconic it became a national joke.

Radio made America feel like one big neighborhood. Whether you were in **New York, Tennessee** (where Evelyn lived), or **California,** you were part of the same national story. Together, we listened to FDR's Fireside Chats. Together, we were fooled—if only briefly—by *The War of the Worlds* broadcast.

Early Television: Susan's Big Day at the Howdy Doody Show

Susan, age five, was thrilled. She was going to be in the audience of the *Howdy Doody* show in New York City. She wore her best dress—a bright red one with white polka dots—and tied matching ribbons in her ponytail. The studio buzzed with excitement. Lights flared. Music started.

Out came Buffalo Bob, followed by a dancing puppet with a freckled face—Howdy Doody himself! Susan was sure he looked right at her. She clapped as hard as her little hands could. The show ended too quickly, but afterward, she got to shake Bob's hand. It was a day she would never forget.

The show, which aired from 1947 to 1960, was a trailblazer in early television. Children in the live audience, like Susan, were proudly called "The Peanut Gallery."

Golden Age of Cartoons

As television found its way into more homes, cartoons became the new Saturday morning ritual. Sometimes, these short clips were even shown before movies in the theater.

When the *Looney Tunes* theme started playing, the children clapped and cheered. These zany characters—Bugs Bunny, Daffy Duck, Porky Pig—made us laugh no matter where we lived. They became part of our shared American experience.

Even now, when Evelyn travels in **Arizona**, she thinks of the *Roadrunner*, the state bird, and his endless outwitting of Wile E. Coyote. *Popeye* taught us that spinach makes you strong, while *Tom and Jerry* turned every hallway into a slapstick chase.

During times when hope and laughter were scarce, cartoons offered both.

More Than Entertainment

Radio and early cartoons didn't just entertain us—they shaped us. They taught us to dream, to imagine faraway places, to believe there was a world waiting beyond our front porch. In many ways, they were our first travels—journeys of the mind and spirit.

As we explore new places today, it's often the characters and cartoons from our past that bring the biggest smiles. They are part of our personal story—the laughter, wonder, and wide-eyed joy that made us fall in love with America in the first place.

SMART TIP: Today, cartoons stream everywhere—from dedicated channels to on-demand platforms. Rewatching them reminds us that laughter is a kind of therapy. Sometimes, a dose of Bugs Bunny or Popeye is just what the mind needs.

Backroads, Washboards, and Jug Music

By Evelyn Kelly

Come with me back into my childhood memories of East **Tennessee**. Every day at noon, Station WNOX aired a program called *The Mid-Day Merry-Go-Round*. One of the stars with the world's best twang was Roy Acuff and his Smoky Mountain Boys. Roy later moved on to Nashville as one of the first performers in the Grand Ole Opry, and today there's even a street in Nashville named after him. But his beginnings were humble in Maynardville, **Tennessee**, where he brought to life such classics as *The Wabash Cannonball* and *The Great Speckled Bird*.

The Cider Jug

Many performers on the program played folk music with whatever they had handy. A big ceramic jug, meant initially for cider or corn squeezin's, became the deep bass of the band. The player pursed his lips and blew across the mouth of the jug, creating a low, steady sound. In skilled hands, that boom-boom thump seemed to vibrate right down into your bones.

The Washboard

Once the weekly washing was done and the lye soap used up, the washboard was pressed into service as a musical instrument. A player might strap on spoons or slip thimbles over each finger, then click, scrape, and rattle out a rhythm that made you want to jump to your feet and dance.

Banjo and Fiddle

Then came melody. The banjo—one of the trickiest instruments to master- strummed along as cheerfully as sunshine. At the same time, the fiddle (never called a violin at these gatherings) was often tucked at the waist so the player could saw away in competition with the banjo. Whether dueling or blending, the pair made magic together.

The Harmonica

Small but mighty, the harmonica could mimic the whistle of a midnight train or carry the haunting lilt of the *Wabash Cannonball*. In the right hands, it could make you dance, cry, or whistle along.

Bottle Music

My husband Charles, raised in South **Mississippi**, often recalled the bottle music of his boyhood. He remembered little boys walking down the railroad tracks, playing music—their hooda-hooda-hooda sound echoing across the rails.

Another form of bottle music involved filling bottles with varying amounts of water. You could tap them with a spoon or blow across the tops, sometimes with a partner adding rhythm. The tones rang out like church bells on a summer morning.

Joyful Music

These bands were never meant for concert halls. Their music belonged on porches, at picnics, or in barn dances, where neighbors clapped and laughed right along with the performers. That was the spirit of the *Mid-Day Merry-Go-Round*—music made from whatever was at hand, but filled with joy.

SMART TIP: Try making your own bottle band! Fill eight bottles with different levels of water and play with them by tapping with a spoon or blowing across the tops. It's a simple, fun project for kids (and grown-ups too).

Joy on Jekyll Island

The Spanish moss hanging from ancient oak trees seemed to wave us toward **Georgia**'s coast and the historic retreat of Jekyll Island—a once-exclusive enclave of the rich and famous. Leaving behind the rumble of I-95, we glided along a quiet paved road, flanked by golden savannahs and sawgrass. A mama feral hog with ten piglets trotted alongside the roadside, as if welcoming us to the wild beauty of the island.

We were on our way, gliding across the causeway and breathing in the salt air, elated to arrive. We thought of General James Oglethorpe, who founded the **Georgia** colony to give debtors and the "deserving poor" a fresh start. What must he have felt upon first setting foot on this promising coast?

A Taste of Coastal Georgia

No visit to **Georgia**'s coast is complete without seafood. We headed to Zachary's Riverhouse, a charming old-style coastal restaurant with an ambiance to match. Being Southerners, we are well acquainted with grits. Natalie and Evelyn chose shrimp and andouille sausage in a creamy sauce served over cheese grits, comfort food at its finest. Sharlene enjoyed fresh blue crab cakes with remoulade sauce and hush puppies. It was a feast worthy of the sea.

Saturday in the Mist

A soft mist settled over the island Saturday morning, but it didn't dampen our spirits. Donning rain gear, we made our way to the Mosaic Museum. There, we explored the island's rich history, from Native Americans and Spanish missionaries to English settlers, French planters, Gilded Age millionaires, and modern-day residents and visitors.

We boarded a tram for a guided tour around the island, captivated by the ranger-historian's vivid storytelling.

Jekyll Island's serene beauty and quiet charm once drew America's wealthiest families. Between 1888 and 1928, the Rockefellers, Vanderbilts, J.P. Morgan, the Pulitzers, and the Goulds built what they modestly called "cottages" alongside a grand clubhouse. This elite community became known as the Jekyll Island Club.

Mark Twain famously coined the term "The Gilded Age" to describe this era, gilded on the outside, hollow within.

At the Jekyll Island Clubhouse—once the private retreat of America's richest families—grand porches and quiet rooms still echo with the stories, secrets, and influence of the Gilded Age elite.

So exclusive was the Jekyll colony that residents arriving by boat from nearby Brunswick were greeted with a shotgun. The press, locked out, ran fanciful stories: that the streets were paved with gold, the houses inlaid with pearls, door knockers were diamonds, and baths were taken in warm milk. Of course, these tales were exaggerated. The cottages, while elegant, were far less extravagant than the grand homes in Newport or along the Hudson.

Festivities

Each January and February, Jekyll Island hosts a beloved treasure hunt, a beachside adventure for all ages. Volunteers known as "Beach Buddies" hide up to 200 clear plastic globes throughout the island's public spots. Find one, and trade it at the Guest Information Center for a stunning hand-blown glass float created by talented U.S. artists.

We loved chatting with the ranger who hides the globes daily—visitors travel from far and wide to join the hunt, and the excitement is contagious.

SMART TIP: Jekyll Island is a national treasure. The preserved "cottages" offer a unique glimpse into America's Gilded Age, especially when contrasted with the more ostentatious homes up North. Come for the history, stay for the salt air, seafood, and serenity.

Stars, Stripes & Holiday Lights: America's Christmas Markets

Why go to Germany to visit Christmas Markets when you can go to Carmel, Bethlehem, or the Great Dickens' Christmas Fair in San Francisco?

A few years ago, our family discussed traveling to Germany to visit a Christmas market. Unfortunately, all tours were full due to the market's popularity.

That's when we discovered that the Christmas market, or Christkindl Markt (German for Christ child market), is celebrated here in the USA. There may be one near you.

Sizzling Sausage and Other Necessities

In 1384, Bautzen, Saxony, was the first recorded Christmas market focused on selling meat and necessities. But over time, items such as seasonal treats, decorations, and crafts were added. The atmosphere became quite festive with singing, dancing, and lots of socializing.

Enter Martin Luther

Martin Luther and the 16th-century Protestant Reformation led to significant changes in the markets. Gift-giving shifted from St. Nicholas Day to Christmas Eve. Instead of Santa Claus, these markets celebrated the Christkindl (Christ Child), who became the central figure, often portrayed by a young girl.

Nuremberg, Germany, and Others

This market is one of the most renowned held on the square in front of the Church of Our Lady. An opening ceremony features Christkindl, a young girl who initiates the activities. Over 180 wooden stalls, with red and white striped roofs, sell everything Christmasy. Today, Christmas markets are a holiday tradition in Germany and have spread to other countries, including the United States.

Christkindlmarkt, Carmel Indiana

You don't have to travel to Nuremberg to experience the magic of the authentic German tradition of Christkindlmarkt. Head to Carmel, **Indiana**. The city, with its offering of 60 huts covered with red and white awnings, is so much like Nuremberg that you think you are there.

Every year, German artisans travel from Erzgebirge, Lauscha, and Oberammergau to craft wood carvings, glassblowing, and more. These artisans create charming works right before your eyes.

The Carmel Christkindlmarkt has been voted the Best Christmas Market in the USA.

Bethlehem Christkindlmarkt

What could be a more suitable place for a Christmas market than Bethlehem, **Pennsylvania**, a city named after the place of Christ's birth?

Join the Bethlehem by Night Motorcoach for a drive through the historic district and the Southside. You see the Moravian Church Settlements, the Bethlehem Heritage sites, and historic Main Street decorated for the holidays.

The Great Dickens Christmas Fair, San Francisco, California

The Great Dickens Christmas Fair covers over 4 acres of the historic Cow Palace exhibition halls. We are immersed in Victorian London, a lamp-lit city filled with hundreds of characters from the imagination of Charles Dickens. It makes you vow with Scrooge in A Christmas Carol, "I will honor Christmas in my heart and try to keep it all year."

Christkindlmarkt Chicago, Illinois

Chicago has a German-style Christmas market that is a fine outdoor experience for the whole family. Appealing to the five senses, a visit to this market is also unique.

Other markets to visit: St. Paul, **Minnesota**, European Christmas Market; Denver, **Colorado**, Denver Christkindlmarkt; Washington, DC, Downtown Holiday Market; Holland, **Michigan**, Kerstmarkt.

SMART TIP: Don't spend thousands of dollars to fly overseas to visit a Christmas market. Take a quick trip to your nearest market in the USA and enjoy Americans selling homemade gifts made by local artisans.

The Mother Who Saved Georgia Football

American football is big. On weekends, fans from sea to shining sea gather to cheer on their teams, reveling in the joy of victory or enduring the agony of defeat. From Pop Warner teams to professional, football is America's sport, but nothing is more exciting than college football. The rivalries are fierce, and the game days are exhilarating with tailgates and pageantry. Nevertheless, when a player is injured, concern transcends rivalry. Fans from both sides clap in encouragement as the player is carried off the field.

No state is more enamored with college football than **Georgia**. The entire South, in fact, has long been known for its passion for the sport. While enthusiasm for football extends nationwide, Southern teams have consistently dominated the field, their rivalries fierce both across state lines and within their own borders.

1897: A Turning Point

Georgia was still recovering from the Civil War and Reconstruction, but the end of the century held promise for renewal. Athletics became increasingly important, not only as a form of recreation but also as a source of pride and vitality for local communities. At the time, **Georgia** boasted three colleges: the University of Georgia at Athens, the Georgia Institute of Technology, and Mercer University. Southern education was on the rise, and athletics played a significant role in that renaissance.

Richard Von Albade Gammon, born in 1879, embodied that spirit. A talented athlete, he attended the University of Georgia and played on the 1896 and 1897 football teams under the legendary coach Glenn "Pop" Warner, the name given to boys' football leagues. Excitement filled the air as Georgia faced off against Clemson, Georgia Tech, and then the University of Virginia for the Southern football title on October 30, 1897.

In those early days, players played both offense and defense. During the second half, as Virginia's runner charged the line, Von Gammon dove into the pile to make the stop. When the players cleared, he lay motionless on the field. Rushed to Grady Memorial Hospital, he was diagnosed with a severe concussion and died the next morning. News of his death spread quickly, devastating fans across the state.

Richard Von Albade Gammon of the University of Georgia gave his life on the football field in 1897, a tragedy that forever changed the game. His death helped spark reforms that made football safer for generations to come.

Public and Political Uproar

Von Gammon's death ignited intense debate. Critics of college athletics argued that such brutal sports distracted from academics and endangered young athletes. The **Georgia** Legislature responded swiftly, passing a bill to abolish college football entirely. The legislation would have eliminated the programs at Georgia, Georgia Tech, and Mercer.

The bill landed on Governor William Yates Atkinson's desk. Should he sign it into law? Passions ran high on both sides.

A Mother's Courage

Rosalind Burns Gammon, Von's mother, was heartbroken by her son's death but understood his deep love for the game. She wrote a letter to the governor. In it, she pleaded against banning football. Young men, she reminded him, died in many other pursuits: skating, climbing, and riding, yet those activities were not outlawed. Her son, she said, would never have wanted football to die because of him.

Governor Atkinson agreed. He vetoed the bill, saving football in **Georgia**.

A mother's letter had preserved one of America's greatest traditions.

Aftermath

In 1921, the University of Virginia honored Von Gammon and his mother with a bronze plaque, now displayed in his hometown of Rome, **Georgia**, a lasting tribute to their courage and compassion.

Safety Efforts Today

Much has changed in the 130 years since that fateful game. Football has evolved from a perilous pastime into a sport grounded in science, training, and technology. Safety is paramount. In Von Gammon's era, players had no helmets, or at best, thin leather ones introduced in the 1920s. Today, helmets are engineered for maximum impact absorption, and concussion protocols are rigorous. Awareness of player health and brain safety continues to grow.

What was once a brutal game has become a highly regulated sport supported by education, innovation, and care.

SMART TIP: Encourage children to participate in organized teams. Structured programs emphasize safety, teamwork, and skill development, values that keep the love of the game alive for generations.

Pirates, Parties, and Legends

Ahoy, matey! If you've ever dreamed of sailing the high seas or shouting "Avast, ye landlubbers!"—now's your chance. Whether you're heading to a pirate party, Halloween bash, or themed cruise, all you need is the right swagger, costume, and attitude to unleash your inner buccaneer.

Pirate Fever Lives On!

Pirate fever never died—it just swapped ships for museums, parties, and film franchises. We've visited several unforgettable pirate haunts and highly recommend these treasures:

St. Augustine Pirate & Treasure Museum (Florida):

The most authentic pirate museum in the world, housing over 800 genuine artifacts that transport you straight to the Golden Age of Piracy. Don't miss Blackbeard's blunderbuss or one of the only three surviving Jolly Roger flags.

The Pirate's House (Savannah, Georgia):

Once an 18th-century inn where sailors and pirates gathered for rum and revelry, local legend says unsuspecting drunks were "shanghaied" through a secret tunnel to waiting ships!

Real Pirates vs. Hollywood Legends

"Pirates of the Caribbean" may make piracy look glamorous, but what was the truth?

- Privateers were legal pirates, hired by governments to attack enemy ships.
- Pirates plundered for their own gain.
- The line between the two was razor-thin, but the consequences were deadly.

Famous Pirates and Their Haunts

Blackbeard (Edward Teach): With his long black beard tied in ribbons, he terrorized the Atlantic coast and blockaded Charleston, **South Carolina**, in 1718. Captured and killed later that year, his legend still looms large along the American East Coast.

The Barbary Corsairs: From the North African ports of Tunis, Tripoli, and Algiers, these pirates plundered merchant ships across the Mediterranean and even captured American vessels after the Revolution. President Thomas Jefferson sent the U.S. Navy and Marines to confront them, launching the nation's first overseas military campaign and inspiring the famous line "to the shores of Tripoli" in the Marine Hymn.

Captain William Kidd: A Scottish privateer commissioned by the English crown to hunt pirates, Kidd crossed the line himself. After years of raiding ships in the Caribbean and Indian Ocean, he sailed to the American colonies, hoping to clear his name. Legend says he buried treasure somewhere along the East Coast before being captured in Boston and sent to London, where he was hanged in 1701. His lost fortune has never been found—fueling centuries of treasure hunts from **New York** to **Connecticut**.

Anne Bonny: Not all pirates were men—some were fierce women. Anne Bonny grew up in Charles Town, **South Carolina**, the illegitimate daughter of a lawyer. Disguised as a boy named Andy, she defied expectations and married a poor sailor against her father's wishes. In Nassau, the pirate capital, she joined Calico Jack's crew—still disguised as a man—and fought fearlessly until capture.

José Gaspar ("Gasparilla"): The legendary pirate of **Florida** folklore may be more myth than man, but his story endures. Said to be a Spanish naval officer turned pirate, Gaspar supposedly terrorized ships along the Gulf Coast, buried treasure on remote islands, and met a dramatic end by wrapping an anchor chain around his waist and leaping into the sea. Tampa celebrates its legacy every year with one of the country's largest pirate festivals, keeping the swashbuckling spirit alive.

From East Coast raiders and fearless women to Gulf Coast legends and real-life battles that shaped the Marine Corps, America's pirate past brims with adventure, rebellion, and bold characters. So, whether you're chasing history or just good fun, it's easy to see why pirates still capture the imagination.

Each year, Tampa keeps the swashbuckling spirit alive at the raucous Gasparilla Pirate Festival, where history and hype collide.
Photo Credit:
La Gaceta newspaper

SMART TIP: If you're exploring the Eastern Coast, plunge into America's pirate past by living it. From Gasparilla in Tampa, **Florida**, one of the nation's largest pirate parades in January, and Beaufort Pirate Invasion in **North Carolina** in November, to the Pirate Fest on Tybee Island, **Georgia**, in October, these festivals turn history into cannon blasts, costumes, and plenty of swagger.

PART 7

The All-American Travel Playbook: Expert Tips for Exploring the USA

"You don't have to cross an ocean to find adventure—it's waiting right here at home."
Evelyn and Natalie Kelly

All-American Way to Travel

Welcome to the All-American Way to Travel, where every journey is shaped around you: your lifestyle, your travel style, and your spirit of adventure.

Traveling across the USA is an adventure, whether you're chasing sunsets on Route 66, dipping your toes in both oceans, or skiing down a stunning mountain slope. But let's be honest: determining when, where, and how to travel can feel daunting, even for experienced travelers. That's where we come in. Drawing on our own cross-country adventures and a few hilarious mishaps and mistakes along the way, we have gathered our best insider tips from three decades of travel and travel friends to make your adventures easier. From packing like a pro to uncovering the quirks of travel hacking, you'll find tricks here you won't see in any blog or search engine.

You will also get to know Evelyn and Natalie, the dynamic mother-daughter duo who have traveled to 89 countries (and counting), every continent, and all 50 states. People often ask about their favorite country, and their answer is always the same: the USA.

Natalie and Evelyn posing with President Roosevelt impersonator. For more than three decades, they have explored the world side by side—traveling to 89 countries, all seven continents, and all 50 U.S. states. As authors and speakers, they share how travel can enhance mental health and even help delay aging. At 91, Evelyn is still setting goals: 100 countries by her 100th birthday. The journey continues.

Red, White & Travel-Ready Quiz

What Type of Traveler Are You?

Every great trip starts with knowing who you are as a traveler. Choose the responses that best match your instincts, then tally them at the end to uncover your traveler type.

1. What is your idea of a perfect travel day?
   a) Waking up in a luxury suite with ocean views and enjoying breakfast in bed.
   b) Wandering a historic old town, antiquing, or eating at a cozy cafe.
   c) Hiking a trail, kayaking, climbing a mountain, or hiking through a forest.
   d) Enjoying festivals, foodie hotspots, or free live music events.
   e) Exploring a museum, historical site, or gallery.
   f) Relaxing on a beach or at a spa with no set schedule.

2. What are your ideal accommodations?
   a) Five-star hotels, spas, or gourmet dining.
   b) Charming B&Bs, cabins, or quirky roadside motels.
   c) A campsite, RV park, or rustic cabin.
   d) Hostels, ecolodge, or motels in the vicinity of festivals.
   e) Book ahead at known hotels.
   f) Hit the road with no set plan or lodging accommodations

3. Your suitcase typically includes:

   a) Designer outfits, chic accessories, and stylish sunglasses.

   b) A cozy blanket, a journal, and a sentimental keepsake.

   c) Hiking boots, a reusable water bottle, and outdoor gear.

   d) A camera, a local guidebook, and room for culinary souvenirs.

   e) Guidebook, notebook, and walking shoes.

   f) Swimsuit, sun hat, and whatever you tossed in at the last minute.

4. On a road trip, you'd prefer to:

   a) Stop at luxury resorts or upscale restaurants.

   b) Visit small-town diners or chat with locals.

   c) Pause at every scenic overlook, national park, or outdoor adventure.

   d) Seek out regional specialties like lobster rolls, tamales, or BBQ.

   e) Tour historic sites, like battlefields or presidential libraries.

   f) Travel somewhere you have never been before.

5. Your dream USA destination is:

   a) Luxury spa in **Hawaii**

   b) A quaint festival in a small town like Havre de Grace, **Maryland.**

   c) Hiking the Grand Canyon or camping in Yellowstone.

   d) A jazz club in New Orleans, BBQ in Austin, or Broadway in NYC.

   e) A Washington, D.C. monument, Boston's Freedom Trail, or Philadelphia's Liberty Bell.

   f) A coast-to-coast Route 66 adventure or wherever the road takes you.

Tally Your Answers:

Count how many times you selected each letter. Your totals will reveal your traveler type. Are you a:

a: Luxury Lover – If your idea of roughing it is running out of room service options, you will adore the USA's indulgent escapes. Picture yourself unwinding at a desert spa in Sedona, **Arizona**, sipping champagne aboard a luxury railcar on the Rocky Mountaineer, or retreating to a beachfront suite in Maui, **Hawaii**. From Napa Valley wine tours to Gilded Age mansions in Newport, **Massachusetts,** this style of travel proves that comfort can be just as exhilarating as adventure.

b: Nostalgia Traveler – For you, travel is about stepping back into simpler times. The USA is sprinkled with small towns that feel like they are right out of a romantic movie. Think rocking chairs on porches in Beaufort, **North Carolina**; walking Old Town Alexandria, **Virginia**; or going back in time to the wild west to Tombstone, **Arizona**.

c: Nature Explorer – Your heart always guides you to the great outdoors. Fortunately, the USA is home to more than 400 national parks and state parks, not to mention endless forests, mountains, and coastlines. You might ride an airboat through the bayous of **Louisiana**'s Atchafalaya Basin, hike the thrilling trails of Zion National Park in **Utah**, or take a scenic float at the base of the Grand Tetons in Jackson Hole, **Wyoming**. From vibrant springs to icy glaciers, arid deserts to lush rainforests, America's natural wonders invite you to explore and embrace its beauty.

d: Culture Craver – Your every trip is a festival of sights, sounds, and tastes. Imagine Mardi Gras parades in New Orleans, **Louisiana**, eating deep-pan pizza in Chicago, **Illinois**, or art walking in Santa Fe, **New Mexico**: the USA is a stage set for your passions for music, flavor, and local traditions, turning every journey into a celebration.

e: History Buff – You travel with a notebook in hand and curiosity in your heart. Walk in the footsteps of presidents at Mount Vernon or stand where Martin Luther King Jr. gave his "I Have a Dream" speech.

Civil War battlefields, Native American heritage sites, and the history of the space race in Cape Canaveral, **Florida**, bring the past alive.

f: Road-Trip Rebel – The open road is your favorite way to travel. Whether taking an RV on Route 66 or tracing the Pacific Coast Highway, you thrive on spontaneity. Your souvenirs are gas station snacks, playlists, and the thrill of not knowing exactly where you will land.

Six Rules for Smooth Travels: Preparing for an American Journey

The number one question new travelers ask us is: "Okay… how do I get started?"

Now that you understand your travel style, it's time to explore six essential rules that will help you prepare for your adventure. These focus points guide you toward confident, informed travel.

Rule 1. Identify the Destination You Want to Discover

Your TRAVEL STYLE quiz results can help point you toward places that match your interests and personality.

Research is key: browse books, travel blogs, podcasts, and social media to identify desired destinations. Tap into the power of word-of-mouth from friends, family, and fellow travelers who provide honest, helpful insights.

Rule 2. Evaluate Your Physical and Financial Readiness

Before committing to an adventure, take an honest look at what your body and budget can comfortably support.

Physical Readiness: Make sure you have the stamina, mobility, or supportive devices needed for the type of trip you are considering. A quick conversation with your doctor can help determine what is realistic and safe. Then, use your TRAVEL STYLE to choose destinations and activities that align with your abilities.

We encourage everyone to travel whenever possible. To support this goal, we created a special section with tips for travelers of all ages, including those with mobility challenges. See page 286 *"How Seniors and Mobility-Challenged Adventurers Can Explore the USA."*

Financial Readiness: Assess whether your current finances align with your dream trip. Travel is rewarding, but expenses can add up quickly, from flights and lodging to meals, excursions, souvenirs, and even pet care. Planning ensures your journey stays stress-free.

For travelers exploring the USA on a budget, we've created a dedicated section on page 283 *Traveling the USA on a Budget.*

Rule 3. Determine With Whom You Want to Travel
Choosing your companions or deciding to go solo shapes the rhythm, pace, and joy of your journey.

Traveling Solo: If you're eager to explore but don't have a companion, don't wait for the "right" time; it may never come. Solo travel is popular, especially among women, and offers opportunities for growth, confidence, and independence.

We've created a special section with tips and guidance for solo adventurers. See page 291 *Traveling Solo: Freedom, Confidence, and Common Sense.*

Traveling with Family or Friends: When heading out with loved ones, set yourselves up for harmony. Talk openly about expectations, interests, budgets, and travel styles. Small planning steps prevent misunderstandings and keep the adventure fun for everyone.

For travelers seeking adventures with children, see page 289 *Traveling the USA with Family and Children.*

Rule 4. Choose Your Preferred Mode of Travel

How you get to your destination influences the experience itself. Do you enjoy the camaraderie of a guided group tour, the relaxed pace of a riverboat, a cruise, or a scenic train ride, or the independence of driving a car or an RV?

Each mode of travel has its advantages:

- Organized tours offer convenience and social connection.
- Cruises and trains allow you to savor scenery without worrying about logistics.
- Flights get you to your destination quickly.
- Road trips or RV adventures offer flexibility to explore at your own pace.

For a deeper dive into each mode of travel, see page 279 for *Choose Your Preferred Mode of Travel: Finding the Best Way to Explore the USA.*

Rule 5. Plan Your Itinerary or Enlist a Travel Agent

Decide whether you want to create your own itinerary or rely on a travel agent. Your choice depends on your travel style, preferences, and how much time you want to dedicate to planning.

Designing Your Own Trip:

Planning your journey yourself gives you complete control, but it also requires research, organization, and time: secure tickets and reservations early, especially for lodging, shows, and restaurants. We've had our fair share of DIY adventures, like the time we booked what we thought was a "charming rustic lodge," only to discover that "rustic" meant no heat and a family of raccoons for neighbors. Needless to say, our next trip involved a travel agent.

But don't let our mishaps discourage you. Plenty of apps can help you find great accommodations and plan your own adventures. Just be sure to conduct thorough research before clicking "Book Now."

The Travel Agent Advantage:
A knowledgeable agent can make your trip seamless and stress-free. They provide insider tips, personalized recommendations, and assistance with accommodations and exceptional experiences. Enlisting an agent combines convenience with expertise, ensuring a smooth, tailored adventure.

Rule 6. Master Your Travel Timing
Coordinating the timing of your travels takes research and thoughtful planning, but the payoff is immense. Check your destination's weather, local events, and peak tourist seasons.

Weather: Consider the climate, seasonal changes, and potential extremes. Knowing what to expect helps you pack and plan activities comfortably. We visited Phoenix, **Arizona**, in August, and let's say we could have fried an egg on the sidewalk!

Local Calendar: Check your destination's calendar for festivals, religious events, sports competitions, wildlife migrations, and school holidays. Timing your visit around these events can create unique experiences and deeper cultural insights: a jazz festival in New Orleans or cherry blossoms in Washington, D.C. We timed our trip to New England to catch the peak of fall foliage.

Tourist Season: Peak periods often bring crowds and higher prices. Traveling during the shoulder or "off-season" can offer a more relaxed, budget-friendly experience.

Bonus Rule: Should Fido Fly or Snooze at Home?
Make the Smart Choice

Traveling with a furry companion can add joy and comfort to any journey if it's the right trip for them. Natalie learned this with her 7-pound Pomeranian, Rio, who happily joined her on more than 20 round-trip flights. Tucked quietly in his travel bag while she worked, Rio was content simply being close to her.

But every pet is different. And every trip is different.

Whether you or your pet struggles with separation anxiety, or your furry friend is more comfortable napping on the couch than flying at 30,000 feet, use this rule to guide your decisions.

For more guidance, flip to *Traveling with Pets: Tips for Happy Tail-Wagging Adventures* on page 294. Let this section help you make the smartest, kindest choice for your four-legged buddy.

A Deeper Dive into Meaningful U.S. Adventures

Now that you've mastered the 6 Rules of Travel, you're ready to dive into destinations and experiences tailored to your unique circumstances. Whether you're exploring solo, traveling with family, adventuring with children or pets, accommodating accessibility needs, or making the most of a budget, this section will guide you toward the perfect American getaway for the way you love to travel.

Choose Your Preferred Mode of Travel: Finding the Best Way to Explore the USA

Traveling is as much about the journey as the destination, and how you move through the world shapes your experience. Let's explore the options so you can choose the one that fits your style.

Organized Tours

From bus tours to river cruises, organized group tours are ideal for travelers seeking a stress-free adventure. Let professionals handle the logistics of your travel while you relax and enjoy the sights.

Perks of organized tours:

- **Convenience:** Flights, hotels, excursions, and dining are all arranged for you, saving time and hassle. Knowledgeable tour directors guide you through the entire tour.
- **Skip the lines:** Tours provide priority access to popular attractions, giving you more time to explore.

- **Structured yet flexible:** While there is a planned itinerary, most tours allow personal time. Just remember: Never be late for departure.
- **Peace of mind:** Experienced companies have safety and contingency plans in place so that you can travel with confidence.

Cruises and Riverboats

For those who love the idea of unpacking once and waking up in a new destination each morning, cruising is pure magic. The rhythm of the water is soothing, and the dining and entertainment onboard make it hard ever to be bored.

Positives of Cruising:

- **All-inclusive ease:** Meals, entertainment, and activities are usually included.
- **Unpack once:** Your suitcase finally gets a vacation, too.
- **Onboard fun:** From social events to entertainment, there's something for everyone.
- **Scenic splendor:** Charming ports create postcard-perfect memories and shopping opportunities.
- **Adventure excursions:** Some of our most memorable experiences have started with a river cruise, like our **Maryland** journey, which included an extended tour of Annapolis and the impressive U.S. Naval Academy. As we stood inside the Academy, listening to the story of how the *Star-Spangled Banner* was written during the Battle of Fort McHenry, a guide opened a window. There, in the distance, we saw the American flag still flying over Fort McHenry while the anthem played. It was a moment that gave us goosebumps. And one we will never forget.

Train Travel

Train journeys add nostalgia, relaxation, and a unique perspective to your travels. We will never forget riding along the scenic **Alaska** landscape, sipping coffee in a glass-dome car as snow-capped peaks glide past.

Why We Love Trains:
- **Scenic routes:** Panoramic landscapes you'd miss on highways.
- **Relaxing atmosphere:** Spacious seats and the freedom to roam make train travel gentle on the body and mind.
- **Eco-friendly:** A sustainable and serene way to see America's beauty.

Air Travel

Air travel gets you to your destination quickly, but a little planning goes a long way toward a stress-free flight. Starting on Page 307 see *Airport: Ready, Set, Board.*

With these recommendations, flying can become a peaceful, even enjoyable part of your journey.

Driving and RV Adventures

Ah, the open road. The freedom to stop when you want. Driving, whether in your own vehicle or a rental, gives total control over your journey.

Road Trip Tips:
- **Know the rules:** Cellphone laws, speed limits, and toll systems vary by state.
- **Plan but stay flexible:** Map key stops while leaving room for spontaneous discoveries.

- **Pack for comfort and safety:** Snacks, water, a first-aid kit, and entertainment make long drives easier. Take regular breaks to stretch your legs.
- **Rental readiness:** Inspect the vehicle thoroughly at pickup and take photos of scratches inside and out, to avoid being unfairly charged for pre-existing damage. Review the fine print for fees, insurance coverage, and mileage limits. Keep ALL receipts for your records.
- **RV adventures:** Reserve campsites early, familiarize yourself with hookups, and check clearance and weight restrictions. Stock up on essentials: water, propane, and safety gear before remote travel.

No matter how you choose to travel, knowing your options and planning your trip transforms it from ordinary to extraordinary. Each mode has its own magic. Pick the one that lets you enjoy every mile of the adventure.

Traveling the USA
on a Budget

Who says you need a large bank account to have big adventures and memories? Some of our favorite times across the USA came from trips where we traded fancy hotels for cottages, or where the best meal was at a local dive, eating on picnic tables with paper plates and plastic utensils.

Here are ways to explore America without breaking the bank:

Use Rewards for free travel

One of the most popular questions for us is how to travel on a budget. Our favorite budget hack is utilizing a credit card with a rewards program. Yes, if you're not using points or miles, you are missing out on free travel opportunities. We turn grocery runs and gas fill-ups into hotel stays and flights, all by collecting loyalty points. Even better, most programs let you pool points with family or friends. Combine your balances, and suddenly you have enough for a round-trip flight. We used our rewards to sit in first class for an overnight flight to Seattle, **Washington**. When we landed, we were rested and ready to roll.

While we charge all purchases to a rewards credit card, we highly recommend paying the entire balance each month to avoid fees.

Know When to Travel

Traveling during the "off season," that window between busy and quiet, extreme crowds and short lines, can save you hundreds. Spring and fall are ideal in most places. For example, you will find smaller crowds at the Grand Canyon if you visit in early April or late October. Lodge rates may drop by up to 30%.

Keep an eye on flight trends and book when prices dip. You could save $100–$200 on a round-trip ticket just by watching the patterns.

Eat Like a Local (only in the USA)

Some of our best meals around the USA have been at local dives and farmers' markets. Eating like a local not only saves money, but it also connects you with the local culture. On the San Antonio River Walk in **Texas**, we enjoyed the most delicious $3 burritos under a starry night and a string of lights while an authentic mariachi band played nearby.

Eating local food on sidewalks only applies to the USA. For more information about eating abroad, see our book, *Have a Love Affair with Travel*. Montezuma's revenge is real and dangerous.

Adventure Doesn't Have to Be Far

Some of the most exhilarating adventures happen right in your own backyard. We call them micro-adventures: short, easy escapes that feed your desire to travel without costing a fortune. Google *"unique places to visit within 100 miles"* of your location and explore a nearby state park, a sleepy small town, or a scenic trail. One of our favorites? A glass-bottom boat ride in Silver Springs, **Florida**. For less than $20 per person, we cruised over crystal-clear springs, spotted remnants from the filming of *Tarzan*, pure beauty, no plane ticket required (at least for us).

Find Your Budget Travel Style

There's no one way to travel affordably. It's all about finding what feels right for *you*.

- **The Luxury Lover:** Boutique hotels or off-season spa deals.
- **The Nostalgia Traveler:** Road trips with friends or vintage motels.
- **The Nature Explorer:** Free trails, camping, or annual National Park passes.
- **The Culture Seeker:** Free outdoor concerts, art walks, or neighborhood festivals.
- **The History Buff:** Smithsonian museums, old forts, or state Capitol tours, many are free.
- **The Road Trip Rebel:** A full tank of gas will take you to your next destination.

How Seniors and Mobility-Challenged Adventurers Can Explore the USA

One of the things we've learned in our travels across America is that adventure knows no limits. This also applies to travelers with physical challenges, thanks to increasing accessibility, innovation, and a nationwide commitment to inclusion.

The dream of travel does not end with age, a diagnosis, an injury, or a wheelchair. In fact, it can be just the opposite, an opportunity to see the world from a new perspective and to discover how capable, resilient, and creative people can be.

America Opens Its Doors

The United States has made tremendous strides in creating a nation where travel is accessible to all. Since the passage of the Americans with Disabilities Act (ADA) in 1990, public spaces, hotels, transportation systems, and attractions have been transformed to welcome travelers of every ability. From national parks with wheelchair-accessible trails to hotels offering roll-in showers, America has become a global leader in inclusive travel.

Rental car companies now provide vehicles equipped with hand controls, some trains offer boarding ramps and accessible cars, and major airlines accommodate mobility devices and service animals. Most major airports have specialized assistance programs to help travelers navigate security and boarding with ease. We have seen this progress firsthand. Evelyn, a frequent air traveler with mobility challenges, requests a wheelchair when booking a ticket. As she arrives at the airport and ticket counter, she is smoothly guided through security and to her gate, and is among the first to board the plane. Upon landing, an attendant is waiting with her wheelchair, ready to assist her through baggage claim. Remember: Don't forget to tip your attendant.

The Great Outdoors for All

The National Park Service has done a remarkable job ensuring that everyone can enjoy America's natural wonders. Many parks now offer paved trails, accessible overlooks, and special programs for visitors with mobility, hearing, or visual challenges. One of our most moving experiences was at Yellowstone. We met a family traveling with their teenage son, who used a wheelchair, following the paved paths to Old Faithful. When the geyser erupted, spraying steam high into the air, his smile said everything. Some parks even offer a free lifetime pass for U.S. citizens and permanent residents with permanent disabilities. It grants free entry to more than 2,000 federal recreation sites.

Tips from the Road

Here are a few lessons we have gathered from conversations and experiences along the way:

Plan: Contact hotels or attractions directly to confirm accessibility. Details matter: door width, roll-in showers, ramps, or elevators.

Use technology: Download applications to find accessible restaurants, restrooms, and public spaces.

Take advantage of local resources: Many cities have accessibility offices or visitor guides.

Ask for Help: Do not be too proud to accept assistance. Americans are generous and willing to help.

Travel with confidence regardless of age or disability by utilizing your travel style:

- **The Luxury Lover:** Seek accessible spa resorts, train accessible sleeper cars, or first-class flights to accessible cities like Las Vegas, **Nevada**, which is known for its wide ramps, smooth sidewalks, and hotels designed with accessibility in mind.
- **The Nostalgia Traveler:** Historic small towns with ADA-compliant trolley tours.
- **The Nature Explorer:** National parks and accessible areas like Cape Henlopen State Park, **Delaware**, which stands out for its adaptive recreation programs, including beach wheelchairs.
- **The Culture Seeker:** Theme parks today are increasingly accessible, with many offering rides and attractions accessible to guests in wheelchairs. Disneyland in Anaheim, **California**, provides excellent ADA accommodations, ensuring that everyone can experience the magic.
- **The History Buff:** Try accessible cities like **Washington, D.C.**, which has excellent public transportation, accessible museums, and even tactile exhibits for the visually impaired. Smithsonian museums have excellent accessibility services.
- **The Road Trip Rebel:** Download applications that map accessible rest stops.

Traveling the USA with Family and Children

Exploring the United States with family is one of the most rewarding ways to see the country. Traveling with children will show you the country through fresh eyes while reminding you to slow down and enjoy the moment. From riding the roller coaster in the Mall of America in Bloomington, **Minnesota,** to the boardwalk excitement of Coney Island in Brooklyn, **New York,** the journey is filled with laughter and sometimes Boardwalk Popcorn.

7 Tips for Family Adventures Across the USA:

1. **Plan around interests, not just destinations:** Traveling to **Indiana** may not be exciting to a young boy, but the Children's Museum of Indianapolis is full of excitement. The "Dinosphere®" exhibit immerses kids in dinosaur times, including a hands-on fossil dig, real fossils to touch, interactive zones, and paleontologists at work.

2. **Mix learning with fun:** Find programs that focus on children that make education part of the adventure: National Parks' Junior Ranger programs, space centers, historic reenactments, and hands-on museums.

3. **Give everyone a voice:** Letting young travelers choose a stop or activity builds ownership and makes them feel like employers, not passengers. This will cut down on "Are we there yet?" complaints.

4. **Keep curiosity alive:** During road trips, encourage them to track your journey by spotting landmarks and following your route on their digital devices. Let them ask questions.

5. **Be flexible:** Some of our best memories came from unplanned detours. Stop at local fairs, scenic overlooks, or quirky signs like in Darwin, **Minnesota**, that say, "Home of the 'largest ball of twine made by one person'."

6. **Laugh through the mishaps:** Flat tires, wrong turns, and rainy picnics all become family legends.

7. **Discover Your Family's Travel Personality:**
    - **Luxury Lover:** Relax at resorts with kids' clubs.
    - **Nostalgia Traveler:** Drive Route 66, stop at baseball games, or revisit places parents/grandparents grew up.
    - **Nature Explorer:** Enjoy National Parks with easy hikes and ranger talks for all ages.
    - **Culture Seeker:** Seek children's museums, music festivals, or family-friendly festivals like Balloon Fiesta, in Albuquerque, **New Mexico**, the largest hot air balloon festival in the world.
    - **History Buff:** Learn at family heritage trips like Ellis Island, **New York**, or Civil War battlefields, or interactive living history museums like Colonial Williamsburg, **Virginia**.
    - **Road Trip Rebel:** Play the "License Plate Game," car scavenger hunts, or take turns picking spontaneous stops.

Traveling Solo: Freedom, Confidence, and Common Sense

There's something empowering about striking out on your own. Whether you're wandering through a small town on a weekend getaway or crossing the country by train, solo travel delivers one of life's most liberating experiences.

Why travel solo?

Solo travel isn't about being alone; it's about being free. It offers independence, meaningful personal growth, unexpected new connections, and quiet, mindful moments that stay with you long after the journey ends.

Safety First

Safety is essential for *everyone* traveling alone, men and women alike.

Top tips:

- **Research before you go:** Know which areas are safe, local customs, and emergency contacts.
- **Stay connected:** Share your itinerary with family or friends and check in regularly.
- **Blend in:** Dress appropriately, avoid flashy jewelry or expensive gadgets.
- **Trust your instincts:** If something feels wrong, walk away.
- **Limit alcohol and stay alert:** Awareness is your best protection.

- **Choose safe accommodations:** Choose reputable, well-reviewed lodgings and use locks or safes.

Smart Tips for Solo Travelers:
- **New to globetrotting:** Start with an organized tour before venturing out alone. This provides structure and builds confidence while introducing you to your destination.
- **Seasoned travelers:** Begin with a local guided tour to learn what to see and where to go before exploring independently.
- **Focus on solo experiences:** Seek travel groups or companies that cater specifically to solo adventurers for support, camaraderie, and unique experiences.

For Women Traveling Alone

Women can and *do* travel solo safely every day, but often face additional concerns. Choose transportation that feels secure, avoid walking alone late at night, and rely on your intuition. Use ride-share apps or hotel-arranged taxis. Connect with other solo women travelers through online groups. Confidence and awareness are your best travel companions.

For Men Traveling Alone

Men may appear less vulnerable, but solo travel carries risks, including scams and unsafe neighborhoods or nightlife. Stay alert, avoid overconfidence, and respect cultural norms, especially regarding dress, behavior, and interactions. Don't flash cash or tech gear.

Destination ideas for solo travel styles:
- **The Luxury Lover:** High-end group tours for safety and pampering.
- **The Nostalgia Traveler:** B&Bs, drive-in movie.
- **The Nature Explorer:** Guided group hikes and women-only eco-adventures.
- **The Culture Seeker:** Foodie tours with built-in social groups.
- **The History Buff:** Historical walking tours with expert guides.
- **The Road Trip Rebel:** Road trip groups.

Traveling with Pets: Tips for Happy Tail-Wagging Adventures

Traveling across the United States is even more enjoyable when you can bring your furry (or feathered) friends along for the ride. With pet-friendly hotels, outdoor attractions, and restaurants welcoming four-legged companions, the U.S. is one of the best countries in the world for pet-inclusive travel. Whether you're hitting the open road or flying cross-country, a little preparation ensures everyone, human and animal, has a safe, comfortable adventure.

So, should you take your furry friend along? The answer depends on your pet's comfort and your travel plans.

7 Tips for Traveling with or without your pets:

1. Plan Ahead: Before you leave home, schedule a visit with your veterinarian. Make sure your pet's vaccinations, identification tags, and microchip information are all up to date, whether you're bringing them along or leaving them at home. If you are traveling with your pet, bring a copy of vaccination records and any medications inside a waterproof envelope. If you're crossing state lines, some areas, like national parks, may have specific health or leash requirements.

2. Health and Comfort on the Go: Pets can experience stress just like people. Keep routines familiar: feed at the same times, bring favorite toys, and offer reassurance. Watch for signs of anxiety or overheating, especially in summer travel. Portable fans, cooling mats, and collapsible water bowls help keep them comfortable. Never leave your dog in a parked car. Temperatures can soar quickly, even on mild days.

3. Road Trip Ready: Most pets love car travel once they get used to it. Keep your pet safely restrained in a secure carrier or a seat-belt harness. Pack essentials: food, water, bowls, leash, waste bags, bed or blanket, toys, and cleaning supplies. We pack all of our furry friends' essentials in a dedicated carry-on bag: easy, organized, and always within reach. Stop every few hours for bathroom breaks and stretches. Many interstate rest areas now have designated "pet zones."

4. Pet-Friendly Stays: Across the country, hotels and vacation rentals are rolling out the red carpet for pets. Major chains have pet-friendly policies, while smaller inns often go out of their way to make your animal feel at home. Be sure to ask about fees, weight limits, or breed restrictions when booking. There are websites that can help you find hotels, restaurants, and attractions that welcome pets.

5. Flying with Furry Companions: If you're flying, research airline pet policies early. Small pets may fly in-cabin under your seat, while larger ones must travel in the cargo area (this can be stressful for animals and is not recommended). Consider nonstop flights and travel during cooler parts of the day to minimize risks.

Natalie became a pro at flying with her small dog and offers the following tips:

- **Approved airline carrier:** Carry your pet in an airline-approved carrier (don't rely on the carrier's claim) that is small enough to fit UNDER the seat in front of you.
- **Identification:** Make sure your pet is chipped, has a collar with identification, and all papers to prove vaccinations.
- **Carrying Case:** Always keep your pet in the carrier case. This keeps your pet safe from any accidental injuries.

- **Security:** Remove your pet from the case while going through security. The case (and collar) will go through the security machine.
- **Snacks:** Bring kibbles and treats in a Ziplock bag, and a bottle to fill inside the airport after security.
- **Layover:** If you have a layover, some airports have designated places for dogs to relieve themselves. If not, you will have to take your dog outside of the airport and return through security to your gate. Therefore, make sure your layover is long enough.
- **Anxiety:** Check with your veterinarian if your pet needs medicine to help reduce anxiety during the flight.

6. Where to Play

The USA is full of adventures perfect for pets:

- **National Parks:** While some have pet restrictions, many allow leashed pets in campgrounds, picnic areas, and certain trails. Check ahead: places like Acadia (**Maine**) and Shenandoah (**Virginia**) are known for being especially pet-welcoming.
- **Beaches: Florida**, **California**, and **Oregon** all offer plenty of dog-friendly, off-leash beaches where pups can romp in the surf. Still, we recommend keeping your pet leashed. Waves, wildlife, and curious beachgoers can make for unexpected adventures you might not want.
- **Cities:** Pet-friendly activities such as outdoor restaurant seating, dog parks, and walking tours are in cities like Austin, **Texas**; Portland, **Oregon**; and San Diego, **California**.

7. Travel Styles with Pets

Your personal travel style can help you pinpoint the perfect destination for you and your furry companion. If you identify with any of the styles below, consider these pet-friendly pairings:

- **Luxury Lover:** Seek out upscale, pet-friendly hotels; bonus points for those that offer spa treatments for pets.
- **Nostalgia Traveler:** Look for classic dog-friendly diners and drive-ins where your pup can join in the retro fun.
- **Nature Explorer:** Head to national parks and preserves with designated dog-friendly trails.
- **Culture Seeker:** Enjoy pet parades, outdoor breweries, and festivals that welcome four-legged attendees.
- **History Buff:** Wander walkable historic districts where your furry sidekick can trot along beside you.
- **Road Trip Rebel:** Hit the open road with the windows down and your dog's tongue happily flapping in the breeze.

Remember: A well-prepared journey makes for happy travelers, both two-legged and four-legged!

Liberty, Luggage, and Logistics: Your Travel Checklist

By this point, your destination, lodging, and transportation should be booked. Now it's time to start preparing for your travels.

A Few Months Out

Stay Connected: Let loved ones know your plans and arrange home or pet care. Create an "In Case of Emergency" notebook with copies of your driver's license, and your full itinerary. Leave a copy with a trusted friend.

Travel Insurance: Protect yourself against cancellations or medical emergencies. When Natalie became ill and cancelled our Arctic Circle excursion in **Alaska**, the insurance company reimbursed the full cost.

TSA PreCheck: Apply early to avoid long airport lines. The interview takes time, but it's absolutely worth it.

Body Boost: Prepare physically for your trip. Begin a walking routine, stay hydrated, and schedule a quick health checkup.

Pet Preparations: If leaving your pet at home, arrange reliable care or lodging. Provide written instructions, vet info, vaccinations, feeding schedules, and any special needs.

Days Before Departure

Organize Essentials: Ensure you have hard copies and digital copies of government-issued ID, tickets, the itinerary, and credit cards.

List of Essentials: Carry a small list of emergency contacts, credit card numbers, and bank phone numbers in your carry-on.

Prescriptions: Refill all medications and pack at least one extra week's supply. List names, dosages, and generic equivalents with your contact list.

Weather-Ready: Check the forecast and adjust your wardrobe. Bring a mini umbrella and a light, water-resistant jacket.

Hideaway Money: Divide cash into two places: your day bag and a locked suitcase or hotel safe.

Credit & Debit Cards: Bring two credit cards. Confirm travel compatibility with your bank and know how to freeze a lost card quickly. For debit cards, load only what you need for the trip.

Keep Receipts: Save receipts, jot the purpose on the receipt, and store them in your luggage. You never know when you'll need proof of purchase.

Stars, Stripes, and Suitcases

Whether jet-setting to a tropical paradise in South Padre Island, **Texas,** or braving the winter in Jackson, **New Hampshire,** selecting the right suitcase is an art form.

Safeguarding Luggage

First, look at ways to safeguard your luggage. Take the following preemptive measures to mitigate the chaos if your bags go astray.

Photo of luggage: Take photos of your carry-on and check-in luggage. Personalize your luggage with unique tags or markings to ensure it stands out in a sea of suitcases.

Hide personal information: Do not display your address for everyone to see. Instead, include your email address on your outer luggage tag and keep your home address inside the luggage.

Travel locks and bands: Secure your bags with TSA-approved locks. We also secure our check-in luggage with locked bands around the bag. We have friends who pull a t-shirt over their luggage, with the handle through the neck. This gives you peace of mind, knowing that your luggage will not open unexpectedly.

Tracking: Secure your luggage with Air Tags for constant surveillance.

Size (and weight) matters: Many airlines have implemented strict size and weight limits for carry-on bags and checked bags. Research airline requirements for bag dimensions and weight restrictions. If your carry-on is too large, you may be required to check your luggage for an additional fee. An extra fee will also be charged if your luggage exceeds the weight limit. We were behind a traveler at the check-in counter who opened his bag and pulled out his underwear and other personal unmentionables to meet the weight limit. Some travelers buy luggage scales; we just use our bathroom scales. At least we are putting our scales to good use.

Pack Like a Patriot

Before you zip up your suitcase and dash out the door, take a moment to set yourself up for a stress-free journey. A little planning on the front end can spare you from airport surprises or frantic searches for missing items.

Handbags and Wallets

Choosing the right bag is essential for stress-free travel.

- **Size:** Opt for a compact cross-body bag. Many museums and attractions restrict large bags, backpacks, and carry-ons.
- **Essentials:** Keep your ID, credit cards, cash, and other payment forms in an RFID-blocking travel wallet.
- **Cell Phone:** Designate a go-to pocket so your phone is always within reach.
- **Must-Haves:** Pack sunglasses, reading glasses, a pocket umbrella, keys, and a small tissue pack. You will thank us in a stall without TP.
- **Wallet Safety:** Never tuck your wallet in your back pocket. Use a slim wallet in your front or zipped pocket and leave unnecessary cards at home.

Carry-On Essentials

Keep these items in your carry-on for convenience and security:

- **Documents:** Tickets, insurance, and itineraries in waterproof envelopes.
- **Clothes:** One change of clothes in case check-in luggage is delayed.

- **Electronics:** Laptop, tablet, chargers, headphones, and cords.
- **Water Bottle:** Bring an empty bottle to fill after security.
- **Toiletries:** Travel-size essentials in zipped bags to prevent leaks: moisturizer, toothpaste, toothbrush, deodorant, hairspray, razor, brush, and comb.
- **Medicine Kit:** Include prescriptions, aspirin, painkillers, cold/flu medication, antacids, allergy medication, anti-itch cream, sunscreen, and any other personal essentials. For families or group travelers, combine resources to create a shared kit.

Build the Perfect Travel Wardrobe

If you've ever overpacked, you're in good company. But building the perfect travel wardrobe is easier than you think.

Follow our **Three-Stage Packing Rule** to stay organized, stylish, and clutter-free.

Stage One: Lay out your clothes early. Consider the weather, season, activities, and cultural norms.Look for clothing that is easy-care and compact, temperature-regulating, moisture-wicking, odor-resistant, and wrinkle-free.

Stage Two: Remove anything you're not 100% confident you'll wear.

Stage Three: Maximize outfits by wearing everything at least twice. Mix and match colors or patterns. For trips over a week, pack:
- Two pairs of pants and two shirts.
- One extra set in your carry-on.
- Rotate outfits creatively so it feels like a new look every day.

With this method, your packing stays organized, lightweight, and stress-free, letting you focus on adventure, not luggage.

Twelve Key
Packing Perfections

When it's finally time to select the clothes and essentials for your trip, follow these twelve key packing principles to stay organized, efficient, and stress-free:

1. Packing Cubes: Keep items organized by rolling similar clothes into cubes. Pack pants in one cube, shirts in another, and undergarments in smaller cubes. Use additional cubes for scarves, socks, and accessories.

2. Jewelry: Do NOT take expensive jewelry. For everyday or custom jewelry, prevent tangles by threading necklaces through cup straws and posting earrings to cotton pads or sticky notes.

3. Undergarments: Pack those older undergarments you've been meaning to toss. Wear them one last time and discard them each night. It keeps your dirty laundry to a minimum, lightens your suitcase, and finally gives you the perfect excuse to replace the ratty pairs you should've retired ages ago.

4. Jackets: Always pack a rain-repellent jacket since umbrellas aren't allowed in some sites.

5. Shoes: Limit yourself to two or three pairs. Closed-toe shoes are preferable. Avoid wearing new shoes for the first time on a trip, or bring plenty of bandages.

6. Shoe Packing Tips:
- Place shoes in a separate bag to protect clothes, or
- Wrap shoes in a hand towel, which can be used for other purposes, or
- Use the suitcase's internal lining: unzip it, tuck in shoes, and zip it closed.

7. Dryer sheets keep clothes smelling fresh and can also be used to repel mosquitoes.

8. Pack a washcloth in a plastic bag; it's a simple luxury, as many hotels now charge for them.

9. Wash clothes in the sink using detergent sheets for multi-night stays. Quick-dry tip: wring water from clothes, wrap them in a towel, wring again, and hang to dry.

10. Water and Sodas: Carry small bottles in zip-lock bags to ensure you stay hydrated and have your favorite sodas on hand.

11. Heavy Bottom: Pack heavier items at the bottom of your suitcase and layer clothing on top to maximize space and balance weight.

12. Do Nots: Never pack valuables in checked luggage. Keep prescriptions, cameras, chargers, laptops, and jewelry in your carry-on.

Airport: Ready, Set, Board

Flying can be stressful, but with a little preparation, you can navigate the airport with ease.

Print Your Ticket: Even if you use an airline app, print a boarding pass as backup in case your phone battery dies.

Arrive Early: Arrive three hours before boarding.

Stay Connected: Download your airline's app for updates. Check in 24 hours before departure. Skip long check-in lines if you have no luggage to drop off.

Airport Check-In: Keep your ticket confirmation or boarding pass handy.

Disabilities: Notify the airline in advance. If you have mobility impairments, airport staff can assist with a wheelchair and help you navigate security and long corridors. Don't forget to tip.

Security: Enroll in TSA PreCheck to breeze through screening. Keep all bag closures fastened to avoid losing personal items, skip belts, and opt for slip-on shoes for easy on-and-off. And before you leave the security area, always pause for a quick double-check to make sure you've gathered everything.

Gate Check: Monitor the flight board for gate changes.

Pay Attention: Boarding times matter. Don't get so absorbed in a book or conversation that you miss your flight.

Flights: Booking and Seat Selection

Flights can feel like a game of strategy: spot the deal, score the seat, dodge the fees. With a little insider know-how, you can turn the whole process into a win. Here's how to outsmart the system and make your journey smoother from takeoff to touchdown.

Booking Tips: Research flights thoroughly; rates fluctuate daily. Mid-week flights often cost less. Watch for extra fees on budget airlines, and allow at least two hours for layovers. Sign up for airline newsletters and deal alerts.

Seat Selection: Book early for the best options. Front seats make boarding and deplaning easier. Bulkhead seats offer extra legroom, aisle seats are ideal for quick restroom access, and seats over the wings reduce motion sickness. Bring any necessary medications.

Seven Ways to Make Flying Fun

Treat your flight like a cozy evening at home.

1. Create a Serene Environment: Keep essentials under the seat in front of you. Listen to music, watch downloaded movies, or meditate to stay relaxed.

2. Wear Comfortable Clothes: Loose, breathable clothing makes long flights more pleasant.

3. Stay Healthy (S.A.M. Approach):
- **Socks:** Wear compression socks to prevent blood clots.
- **Agua:** Drink plenty of water.
- **Move:** Walk or stretch every two hours. Keep skin hydrated with moisturizer.

4. Combat Jet Lag: Adjust your watch to your destination's time upon boarding. For red-eye flights, consider a light sleep aid and an eye mask to block light.

5. Bathroom Safety: Always wear shoes; puddles are not water.

6. Landing Comfort: Open your mouth to equalize ear pressure.

7. Disembark Etiquette: Wait for those in front of you before leaving the plane.

Hotel Hacks

Make your stay smoother, safer, and more rewarding with these tips:

Maximize Rewards: Join hotel loyalty programs or use a hotel credit card to earn points for free stays. Keep your rewards number handy and ask about upgrades. If the hotel isn't full, they often accommodate requests.

Secure Your Room: The first things Natalie does when entering a hotel room are twofold: 1) she checks that all windows and doors are locked, and 2) she hangs the "Do Not Enter" sign outside the door. For extra security, especially when traveling solo, consider using a portable door lock or stopper. Always lock your luggage and store valuables in the in-room safe.

Don't Forget Items: Natalie keeps all personal items in a designated area. The more you spread clothes and belongings around the room, the easier it is to leave something behind. She also places a piece of paper in front of the refrigerator as a reminder of any drinks or food she has refrigerated there.

Be Emergency-Ready: Keep a robe, coat, and shoes within reach. We learned this the hard way in Boston, **Massachusetts**, when a fire alarm went off in the middle of the night. Heading outside unprepared was a cold lesson in travel readiness.

Conclusion

With fresh insights and a greater appreciation for the richness of our country, may we continue to explore the USA with curiosity, respect, and an open heart. Let every journey be an opportunity to learn, connect, and celebrate the diverse stories that make this nation remarkable. As one adventure comes to a close, may your excitement for the next journey grow. Here's to discovering, embracing, and falling in love with the USA, one unforgettable adventure at a time!

Natalie and Evelyn are honored to receive the 2025 International Impact Award for their first book, *Have a Love Affair with Travel: Your Ticket to an Exhilarating Life.*

Acknowledgments

With full hearts, we extend our deepest gratitude to the many people who helped bring *Have a Love Affair with the USA* into the world. This book did not grow from words alone; it grew from shared moments, honest conversations, and open doors we encountered across the country. Every mile we traveled and each person we met added something to this journey. To all who encouraged, inspired, and cheered us on, whether briefly or over many years, thank you. Your spirit lives in these pages.

We are especially grateful to our first (and bravest!) beta readers, who read all 78 stories and offered thoughtful, honest feedback. Our heartfelt thanks go to Patricia Nevard, Dr. Kevin Singer, Dr. Casius Pealer II, Gwynn Pealer, Daniel Dean, Nickie Zenn, Ed.S., NCSP, Mary Keip, and Sharon Prinze. Your insights strengthened this book in countless ways.

Our gratitude also goes to those who shared their personal stories or took the time to be interviewed: John Hile, Mike Hile, Dr. Kevin Singer, Margie Howard, Susan Pitsche, Suan Grant, Cindy Perfico, Rich Ramos, Paul Bebee, and Valerie Gledhill. Your voices added depth and richness that we could never have created on our own.

Thank you to Senior Learners, Inc. at the College of Central Florida, and to Master the Possibilities at On Top of the World in Ocala, Florida, for inviting us into your learning communities. Your support has meant more than you know.

Our sincere appreciation goes to our travel agent, April Powell of Ocala Travel, whose expertise has guided us through decades of adventures—89 countries, all 50 states, and every continent. Her steady wisdom helped bring our love of lifelong travel to life.

To our family, thank you for your endless encouragement. And to big sister Sharlene Chatham—thank you for your ideas, articles, thoughtful advice, and your belief in this project from the start.

We are also grateful to the team at authorsuccess.com—especially Steve Harrison, Cristina Smith, Christy Day, and everyone involved—for their guidance and enthusiasm. They helped turn our first book, *Have a Love Affair with Travel*, into a bestseller and award-winner, and their support laid the foundation for this companion book about the USA.

Picture of Febb and Harry Burn—Used by permission "Harry T. Burn papers McClung Historical Collection".

Disclaimer: The stories and travel tips in this book are based on our own experiences or shared with us graciously and with permission.

About the Authors

Evelyn Kelly, a resident of Ocala, Florida, is a writer, speaker, and teacher. She holds a Ph.D. from the University of Florida, a master's degree in religion, and a Bachelor of Arts degree from the University of Tennessee. Her education and interests are diverse. Her undergraduate studies included microbiology, English, and history. Evelyn has written twenty-two books on such topics as stem cells and a two-volume encyclopedia of genetics. Evelyn has taught at four universities. She speaks and writes on travel topics, including a popular series called "Armchair Adventures."

Natalie Kelly is an accomplished writer and the Chief Executive Officer of a prominent state organization, residing in Tallahassee, Florida. She holds a Master of Science in Communications and a Bachelor of Science in Visual Arts, with a concentration in Art and Art History, from The Florida State University.

With a distinguished career spanning over thirty-five years in government affairs at the state and national levels, Natalie has held several notable positions, including serving as the youngest female director in the Florida Senate and as a director in Washington, D.C. She was the owner of a successful public relations and lobbying firm.

In addition to her executive leadership, Natalie contributes op-eds to various newspapers and is a sought-after speaker on a wide range of topics. Her expertise and insights continue to influence and inspire audiences across different platforms.

Evelyn and Natalie are a mother-daughter travel and writing team. They have traveled to seven continents, eighty-nine countries (and counting), and all fifty states.

You can learn more about their travels or reach them to book speaking engagements at their website: www.travelersatheart.com.